D0901734

Why Would Grandma Move To *Alaska* ?

By

DeVonne Koppenberg

With Illustrations
by

Tom Schleicher

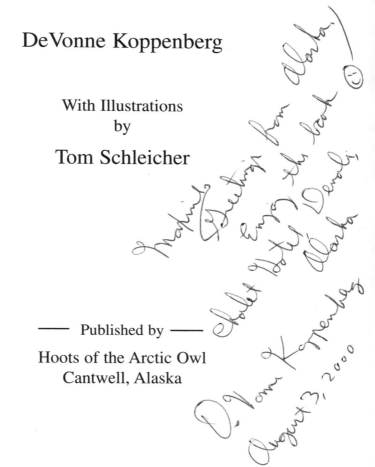

—— Published by ——

Hoots of the Arctic Owl
Cantwell, Alaska

Acknowledgement

I am grateful to my wonderful husband Jerome, who made this book possible.

A special thanks to Bernd and Susan, who inspired me to write this book, to Nita Rosauer, and to Steve Atwater for their time spent proofreading and editing. To my son Tom, for his art work. To Chris Bodick, Doug O'Brien, Chris and Len Sawyer, Ellen Wycoff, and Bernd Richter for their technical assistance.

––––––––––––––––––––––

Requests for permission to copy any part of this publication are to be mailed to: Hoots of the Arctic Owl
DeVonne Koppenberg
P.O. Box 170
Cantwell, Alaska 99729

First paperback printing 2000
ISBN 1-57833-117-X

About the cover:
Photo of DeVonne and Jerome Koppenberg at their home at Colorado Lake, Cantwell, Alaska, taken by Tom Schleicher, July 1998.
Photos: All photos in this book were taken by the author unless otherwise stated.

All mistakes are solely mine.

In Memory of
Joe, Amanda, and Evan
Missed forever

৻৶

TABLE OF CONTENTS

Part 1

Part 2

Introduction

I was startled awake from a nap on the afternoon of June 17, 1998, when my husband, Jerome, tapped me on the shoulder and pointed to the picture window, I turned to look at the window as I sat up. To my surprise there by the big window was a black bear. It had its paws on the glass, one on each side of its head. The bear swayed side to side as it looked into the house. I jumped up and said, "Get the cameras, get the cameras." Jerome and I grabbed our cameras and began snapping pictures.

The bear was at the window for only a couple of minutes. As the bear started to go down on all fours, Jerome opened the door to frighten it away. When it was leaning on the window we could tell that pressure of its weight could cause the glass to break. Jerome yelled at the bear and it made "woof-woof" sounds as it scurried off the deck and into the woods.

The bear left a paw print on the window that remained there for over a year. I couldn't bring myself to wipe it off. That paw print was a reminder of our surprise visitor. The bear did not frighten us, the incident made good conversation while showing off the finished photos.

My camera produced two excellent photos of the bear. Jerome's camera malfunctioned and he did not get any pictures. To his disappointment the film had not engaged on the reel, so it had not advanced.

Bear by our window, June 17, 1998

Same bear leaving

PART ONE

Chapter 1

I am often in awe of my surroundings and I am fascinated with the life style in Alaska. Alaska, however, has not always been my home. This adventure set root in August of 1991. With two of my children Sandy and Tom Schleicher ages 17 and 14, (their father died in 1978). We were enjoying a camping trip along the North Shore in Minnesota and into Canada. One of us asked, "What will we do next year for vacation?" Then one of us said, "Let's go to Alaska." None of us remembers who made those comments. Our conversation was sparked with the exciting idea of going to Alaska. As the idea became more and more intriguing, we thought seriously about it.

During the next few weeks we told family and friends about our plans to visit Alaska. Some were fascinated with the idea and encouraged us. Others were more doubtful. The idea of this being a possibility became more and more evident. We began our planning in earnest. The more we talked about our trip to others caused us to realize that if we were saying we were going to Alaska we had better carry through with our plan. This set our planning in full swing.

It took nine months of planning to actually prepare for this adventure. When we bought groceries we watched for sales on dry packaged food items such as instant cereals, soups, cocoa mix, as well as rice, macaroni, and powdered milk. In my food dryer I dehydrated bananas, apples, mushrooms, as well as some vegetables. I also made fruit leathers and beef jerky. Well cooked hamburger dehydrated quite nicely. Some of these items were successfully used in combination with macaroni and rice. The dried thin sliced lunch meat, however, was not a hit. It was referred to as "birch bark" whenever it appeared in a meal. It wasn't very tasty and it was tough to chew.

We had agreed that food wasn't going to be a highlight of our trip. Our meals would provide nutrition, but nothing more. We also took vitamins with us. Fresh foods were not common items. We did on occasion purchase potatoes, bread, fruit, or some vegetables, but these were treat items not a staple in our diets. When packaging our food items we used disposable containers, boxes and bags. When something was used up we discarded the container. Therefore, we gained space when items were used up, providing more room and comfort in the van.

By taking our food with us we cut down on expenses. During our two month trip from Minnesota through the northern states into Canada and Alaska we didn't eat in a cafe more than half a dozen times. Laundry was another expense we managed to avoid, for the most part. We washed our socks and underwear while showering. We wore our clothes until they obviously needing laundering. We went to a laundromat twice during our trip. One time we hung our clothes to dry on a shelter, the van, and rope we strung up, in a camping area. It was amazing that two teenagers agreed to wear their clothes for an extended time.

We picked berries to add to pancakes. This was a nice treat. One evening Tom was picking strawberries. I had told him to put them in the van so we could have them the next morning in our pancakes. I didn't want him to bring them into the tent where they might spill.

A short time after he began to pick the berries, Tom came stumbling into the tent. I immediately reacted in haste telling him he was to take the berries to the van, not into the tent. Tom said, "But Mom, I was picking strawberries, looked up and a wolf was watching me and the tent was closer than the van!"

Sandy was in the van, she also saw the wolf. I didn't, by the time I got out of the tent to look the wolf was gone.

We had two tents with us. One was enclosed, the other a screen tent we put over picnic tables at camp sites. We used the screen tent when we stayed in a camping area more than one night. It wasn't easy to put up, therefore, we did not use it everyday.

Each of us had designated duties, this worked out quite well. I did all the driving, being the only licensed driver, Tom kept a log of miles, gas purchases, oil changes, and other expenses. We traveled about 11,800 miles during our two month trip.

Sandy's job was housekeeping. She kept track of all our food items. Each night she cleaned out and straightened up the stacked storage bins to keep it all in order. She also helped with some of the cooking. We all did our duty turn washing dishes.

Tom was our expert at making camp fires. He was a Boy Scout and had learned several different ways to build different types of camp fires. He was always anxious to show us a different style of camp fire for cooking. The type he would build depended on the wind, weather, and location. Tom was also the main cook. We had preplanned menus while preparing for our trip, so we had a flexible guide to choose from. Tom and

13

Sandy each kept a journal of our trip. Sandy kept a list of where and when pictures were taken. We took about 300 pictures.

During the planning stage of our trip I purchased *The Milepost*, the most important book for an Alaskan visitor. I also had an array of maps and brochures. I had highlighted the map to Prudhoe Bay, Alaska, which is on the northern coast of Alaska. We had maps taped to our living room wall, we would look at them and try to imagine what it would be like in Alaska. The three of us continued to plan our trip. As the time neared for departure our excitement heightened.

The following is a list of items we took with us:

Macaroni and Cheese	6 boxes
Canned Spaghetti	3 cans
Canned Whole Chicken, Jar of Instant Coffee	
Package of Soup Noodles, Small Sack of Rice	
Bacon Bits	
Canned Tuna	5 cans
Onion Soup Mix	3 packages
Bag of Carrots, Dried Meat	
Spices, Seasons, Sugar and Salt	
Small Packs of Catsup, Mayonnaise and Mustard	
Potatoes I Dried	3 quart-size bags
Dried Mushrooms	About a pint
Dried Chipped Beef (referred to as birch bark!	1 quart-size bag
Small Jar of Peanut Butter	
Small Container of Parmesan Cheese	
Box of Dried Whipped Topping Mix	1
Textured Vegetable Protein Mix	6 cups
Popcorn (used shaker-type, over campfire)	1 pound
Self-dried Apples, Kiwi, and Bananas	4 quart-size bags
Fruit Rolls (leathers I made)	
Apple and Cherry Pie Filling	2 cans each
Powdered Drink Mix	2 large cans
Marshmallows	5 small bags
Girl Scout Cookies, Graham Crackers	1 box each
Rye Crisp Crackers	1 box
Rice Cakes	2 bags
Canned Fruit Cocktail and Mandarin Oranges	3 cans each
Hot Cocoa Mix	60 single-serve

	packs
Hot Cider Mix	30 single-serve packs
Powdered Milk	1 pound box
Flour	About 2 pints
Macaroni and Rice Prepared Meal Mixes	4 each
Instant Potatoes	1 large box
Gravy Mix	3 packages
Margarine	1 squeeze bottle
Cooking Oil	1 quart
Pancake Mix (add water, mix and pour)	8 containers
Syrup1 pint	
Ready-Made Pudding (individual cans)	three 6-packs
Sardines	4 cans
Chocolate Candy Bars	4
Christmas Candy (hard)	1 bag
Aluminum Foil	2 small rolls
Plastic Wrap	1 small roll
Laundry, Dish Soap, Bar Soap and Shampoo	
Rags , Towels and Scrubber	
Pots, Pans, Dishes, Cooking and Eating Utensils	
Cups, Glasses- Bare Minimum, Dish Pan	
Bug Spray, Aspirin, Septic Stick, First Aid Kit	
Mosquito Head Net	3, we never used
Camp Stove, Water Jug, Rope	
Camp Stove, Lantern, Fuel, and Matches	

Glue Stick, Writing Paper, Pen, Envelopes, Addresses and of course our cameras and 15 rolls of film.

With our pre-made menus we had enough food, it worked out quite well.

Chapter 2

We left home, in Alexandria, Minnesota on June 7, 1991. With our van packed full, we headed out ---- to **Alaska**! Our first day took us into North Dakota, the next into Montana where we spent our second night. During the night a rain storm drove us from our tent to the van. Our tent and bedding got wet so we were faced with the task of drying out our things the next morning.

It was sometime after leaving Glendive, Montana, that Sandy and Tom saw mountains for the first time. Sandy had thought one could just drive up to a mountain, such as a hill or lake. She did not realize the vastness of them and that mountains can be seen a hundred miles or more away.

We arrived at Prince Rupert, British Columbia, where we got an oil change in the van. Here Sandy and Tom saw the ocean for the first time. A first for all of us was seeing a glacier, Bear Glacier, near both Stewart, British Columbia and Hyder, Alaska. We marveled at the blue color and its beauty.

We camped at Stewart, British Colombia, on the nineteenth of June. The next day we traveled two miles and were in Hyder, Alaska. We could not drive beyond Hyder because the roads were not all plowed. These two little towns, Stewart and Hyder were nestled in the beautiful Lincoln Mountains.

We drove back into British Columbia, then into the Yukon before we could get to the main part of Alaska.

Throughout Sandy's journal she wrote her entries at night, commenting on the length of the daylight, that increased as we continued north. Most of the account about our trip to Alaska was taken from Sandy and Tom's journals.

Watson Lake in the Yukon Territory was the location of Sign Post Forest, where more than 10,000 signs of all types were put up by travelers over the years. We did not have anything to make a sign out of, so we used a piece of white terry cloth towel. We wrote on it with a black marker, somehow without nails or a hammer, we managed to hang it among the other signs. Most of these signs had peoples names, addresses, dates, and perhaps a comment about their travels, written on them.

June twenty-fourth, was an exciting day for us. We finally crossed into Alaska, besides Hyder, this was actually getting further into the state. At our first camp site in Alaska, we went for a walk at midnight and were amazed at how light it was. It was possible to read in the tent, without a lamp, at anytime during the night and early morning. It was light around the clock at this time of the year.

June twenty-fifth, we camped in Fairbanks, a man in a near by camp site gave us a nice piece of halibut, a welcome change from our food. After we left Fairbanks, a few miles north, we saw our first moose, there were four of them. We were excited at the sight of these large, awkward looking creatures.

Sandy and Tom wanted to go to a hot springs. We left

Fairbanks drove, sixty-two miles to a hot springs. When we got there it was closed. We then drove back to Fairbanks, looked in our literature and found one, at Manley Hot Springs. Manley Hot Springs is located 152 miles from Fairbanks at the end of the Elliott Highway, which begins ten miles north of Fairbanks. The last eighty-three miles of the Elliott Highway was narrow and crooked, which made driving slow. We enjoyed our stay at the hot springs, swimming in the warmed pool, spending the night and swimming again the next day. From there we drove further north across the Arctic Circle where we took pictures. Later we arrived at Cold Foot, which is the northern most truck stop. There we were each given a certificate with our name on it verifying we had crossed the Arctic Circle. We set up our camp site and spent the night at Cold Foot. Leaving there the next morning June twenty-ninth, at about 10:30 A.M. we headed north on the Dalton Highway, destination, Prudhoe Bay. Prudhoe Bay is an oil drilling port at the northern most part of Alaska. Here the oil is piped about 800 miles to the south, to Valdez, Alaska.

Arriving at Prudhoe Bay at 7:30 P.M., we stopped for gas, I inquired about a place to stay. The lady at the station told me we had better leave, because if we were caught on the road without a permit we could be fined $500.

I paid for the gas and we headed back out of town. That gas receipt was the only souvenir we got in Prudhoe Bay. I purchased $18 of gas at $1.77 a gallon. I did take a picture of the Dalton Highway sign, on our way out of town.

Both going to and from Prudhoe Bay we stopped once each way to eat. There were no places, other than turn-outs along the road, to stop. The road was very dusty, only large trucks used that road, also called the Haul Road. Truck drivers did not always look favorably upon other traffic on the road.

The times we stopped to eat, we would set up our camp stove beside the van and fix something to eat. All the while watching in both directions for big trucks. When we saw one, several miles away, we had time to get our things put back into the van and get back inside before the truck got to us. The dust was very thick so we did not want to get caught in it.

While driving, I often had to stop and decide if I wanted to hit the hole or the rock. This entire road was a dirt road and quite poor for a car to travel on.

We were not stopped or fined. I realized we were driving on a restricted road, but took the chance anyway. Since our trip there the road was opened to the public, in December, 1994. I do not know if it is in any better condition since we traveled it, but I hear tourist still aren't a welcome sight on the road.

The scenery was spectacular on this eighteen hour, practically non-stop 244 mile round trip. We saw a rainbow in the Brooks Range Mountains about 2:30 A.M., the morning of June 30.

Checking in Sandy's journal, she wrote that on July second, we ate in a cafe, that was really good, after nearly a month of camp cooking.

July ninth, we took a bus trip into Denali National Park. We got to see caribou, moose, Dall sheep, and bear, all quite far away. The trip took us as far as Eielson, a place to stop, observe the scenery, perhaps see animals, as well as interesting information about earthquakes. We heard about busses that went even further on the Park Road to Kantishna (later we couldn't remember the name, Kantishna), but it was expensive. It was an overnight trip on a special bus. We often talked about going to where the other bus went, saying it sure would be neat to see what was further in the Park. This intrigued us, especially me.

While in this area of Denali National Park entrance, Tom went on a helicopter ride near Mt. McKinley. He really enjoyed that trip, having never been in an helicopter before.

We all went white water rafting on the Nenana River which was near the Park. That was exciting, the water was rough and very cold, about thirty-six degrees. The ride was about eleven miles long. Photographers took pictures of us from shore that we later purchased. The pictures revealed the excitement on our faces, of this wild ride.

As we continued our travels, we drove to the Matanuska Glacier on the Glen Highway east of Palmer, Alaska (another name we later could not remember or pronounce.) We camped near the glacier. The following morning we hiked out on the glacier, for two and half hours. On our way back to our camp site, we took a different route. Sandy and Tom got across a small stream without any problem, I did not, however. On the opposite side from me were four young men. I attempted to talk to them thinking perhaps they knew a better way for me to cross. I soon realized they were all Japanese and could not speak English. Finally I said, "Help." They all nodded their heads to indicate they understood me.

As I started across, by stepping on the slippery wet rocks, I fell into the icy shallow water. I had no sooner got into the water when these men grabbed my hands and quickly pulled me out of the water. I was very thankful for their assistance. My biggest problem, however, was to get them to understand that I wanted a picture of them. After sometime I was successful, Tom and I stood with them while Sandy took our picture.

From the Matanuska Glacier we drove the beautiful drive to Valdez, Alaska. This is where the pipe line ended coming from Prudhoe Bay. We felt we had made quite and accomplishment, having driving nearly the entire length of the state. Valdez has State Ferry systems picking up passengers to travel to Juneau, Cordova as well as other locations. In Valdez I put the van on a ferry. We boarded the 193 foot, 170 passenger, thirty-eight vehicle ferry bound for Cordova, Alaska. We arrived in Cordova at 5:00 A. M. on July seventeenth. Of course we did not know a soul there or where to go. As we were driving around town a lady saw us and stopped to talk to us. I told her we were trying to find a place to stay or camp. She didn't know where we could camp, but she said if we needed a place to stay we could stay at her church. That was nice of her to offer. She said she saw the Minnesota license plates, a woman with two kids, and thought perhaps we needed some assistance.

We spent two hours in a state office trying to get a cabin that was located outside of town and run by the state. The cabin was usually booked full, but the computer wasn't working properly, so the lady could not tell if the cabin was occupied. She told us to drive out to the cabin, twenty-two miles, and if there wasn't anyone there we could stay. We drove out to the cabin and found two young men traveling by bicycle were using the cabin. They told us they would gladly share it with us, we declined. We returned to the same office, they then found us a bed and breakfast in town, overlooking the ocean.

July 18 we went from Cordova to Childs Glacier. We were amazed at the huge glacier. It was fascinating to see the large pieces of glacier break off, called calving, into the Copper River. When these fell and hit the water it sounded like a loud gun shot. We observed this from a special observation deck across the half mile of river to the glacier. There was a path along the river which we walked on. On this path were rocks and large sticks that had landed on the pathway from the river when glacier ice fell into the water. Walking on this path was at one's own risk, because of the danger of being hit by rocks and sticks. I wondered if fish were ever forced out of the river by the ice chunks?

The Million Dollar Bridge, named for the cost of its construction in 1909 and1910, was visible down the road. We drove to the bridge then across it. Part of the bridge was in the Copper River, as a result of the Good Friday Earthquake in 1964. A wooden ramp bridged the gap to enable traffic to cross. It was scary, but we drove across just to say we did!

About midnight we returned to the loading area to board the ferry back to Valdez. I did not want to be late, thinking if I didn't get there early perhaps there would not be room on the ferry for our van. Well, I learned my lesson on being first in line. Being first meant I had to back the van the entire length of the ferry to park in the far end! It wasn't easy to back that length down a narrow restricted area.

During the ferry trip back to Valdez, Sandy got to go up into the pilot's house to watch the crew pilot the ferry. She enjoyed that, it was an exciting experience for her. She had to leave when large ice floes were seen in the ocean.

We arrived in Valdez at 5:00A.M. Not being able to find space in a camp ground we went to a nice bed and breakfast outside of town. There we rested up for our ocean fishing trip scheduled for the next day.

At 7:00 A.M. July 20, we met Jerry Gustafson and his son Olaf at the dock to go fishing on his boat, Gusty. It was a clear, calm, beautiful day. Valdez is often rainy, so we were lucky to have such a fine day.

On the way to the place we were to fish we observed another boat with smoke rising from one end. Jerry contacted them to see if they needed assistance. We thought we were in for a rescue, but they had just burnt a belt on an engine, luckily it wasn't serious. It took an hour to get to the place Jerry wanted us to fish, in Prince William Sound. The sea lions provided entertainment for us as they romped around on and off the buoys floating in the water.

Excitement struck when Sandy caught a 72 pound halibut. Tom and I brought our lines in to be out of her way. When Tom brought his line in he had a five pound cod. Hardly worth mentioning compared to the halibut. Jerry harpooned the fish and stunned it with a club so he could get it into the holding tank of the boat. Several hours later the halibut began to thrash around. The large fish made a lot of noise as it flopped around in the holding tank. But the fish was well contained and did not cause any problems.

When we returned to Valdez, twelve hours later, after taking lots of pictures, Jerry cleaned the fish. Halibut is a peculiar flat fish that is white on one side and black on the other. Jerry showed us where one eye had traveled from the white side to the black side, so both eyes were then on the black side, as they are bottom feeders. This fish swims white side down. A scar-like indention was visible after this strange process had taken place during the maturing of the fish. He gave us the choice part of the cheek to cook that night. After the fish was cleaned there was 45 pounds of meat. We kept the fish on ice in our cooler until the next morning when we took it to the fish exchange. The fish exchange took the halibut, cut, and wrapped it, then froze it. We also had some of it smoked. They mailed it to us when we returned to Minnesota, shipping it on dry ice.

While in Valdez we decided to treat ourselves to a pizza. We found a place that looked good to us. We went in and sat down. The waitress brought us each a large glass of water, then handed us large menus. Tom was sitting across from Sandy and me. I was holding my menu and looking at it when Tom picked up his menu, and as he raised it up, it caught the edge of my glass of water. Water splashed on me and all over the table. I reacted by yelling and stood up! I was startled as my lap became drenched with cold water. Tom lowered his menu and looked at me as if to say, "what's wrong with you?" He did not know what had happened! I had to eat my pizza as I sat in my wet clothes, but we enjoyed the delicious pizza.

July 24, one month to the day of arriving in Alaska, we left going back into the Yukon. As we left we all expressed the desire to return perhaps live in Alaska someday. Two days later when we were again in Watson Lake, Yukon Territory, we checked to see if our towel-sign was still there. It was.

On our way back to Minnesota, we often stayed in camp grounds that we had stayed in on our way to Alaska. On August 7, 1991 we got back to Minnesota. We were anxiously greeted by my daughter Cheryl and her family. We were more than eager to tell everyone about our most fascinating trip to Alaska.

Dall sheep, Dalton Hwy., June 29, 1991

DeVonne and Tom with Japanese, Matanuska Glacier, July 16, 1991. Tom is at the far right and DeVonne is fourth from the left.

Jerry, Sandy and Olaf with halibut, July 20, 1991

24

Chapter 3

Following our vacation trip to Alaska I enrolled in Fergus Falls Community College, which meant returning to school after thirty-three years. School had not been high on my list of enjoyments. But I was willing to give college a try. When I returned to Alaska I wanted to have an education so I could get a good job. Elementary education was my interest.

When I called the college I remember Donna Tollefson answering the phone. After I told her of my intentions of possibly going back to school, she was quick to tell me I had called the right place and to come in the following week.

Shortly after returning to Minnesota I was visiting with some friends, Eddy and Darlene Bussmann, at Melrose. I was excited as I related our trip to my friends. At that time I had not told anyone about my desire to return to Alaska. During the conversation Eddy said to me, "You're going back, aren't you?" I was surprised at his comment. How right he was. His tone was like--he had it all figured out. Most of my family and friends were skeptical of my plans when they heard Tom and I were going back. My dear friends Carl and Diana Ilgen did not doubt that I would return to Alaska. I believe they were the only ones who were really excited for us. Others sort of took the wait and see approach.

The next two years required me to drive from Alexandria, Minnesota to Fergus Falls, Minnesota a 100 mile round trip, every school day. Traveling was not always easy. I remember snow storms out on the flat prairie when the snow blew across the interstate highway reducing visibility to a few feet. Likewise, in milder weather, fog was often a problem causing reduced visibility.

During these two years I had nearly perfect attendance. I was determined to be there and succeed in my courses. I thoroughly enjoyed school. Besides myself at home, I had two teenagers attending high school in Alexandria.

Graduation at Fergus Falls Community College was on June 5, 1993. I had completed my general courses. During the previous two years Tom and I decided to move to Alaska before I finished getting my degree. I would have to attend another college or university in order to take further education courses.

There was a great deal of preparation to be done before we could move to Alaska. I contacted the University of Alaska Fairbanks and worked with them on getting enrolled, classes picked out (some later needed to be changed), as well as applying for student housing and establishing a mailing address at the university, among a number of other things. All this took several months of work while I was attending college in Minnesota.

My friend Chleo Anderson, had a yard sale at which many of our things were sold. We gave things away and threw away those things one keeps thinking there may be a use for some day.

We carefully decided what was necessary to take with us. With that came the task of further condensing to get it all into

26

the minivan as well as two cargo carriers on top.

Tom used string, after measuring the inside dimensions of the van, to recreate the same size in our living room. He then placed our larger items in that space. Among the things were, two TV sets, cedar chest, trunk, ping-pong table, dinette set (disassembled), two chairs, microwave, besides smaller items, clothes, camping equipment, personal items and food.

A large oil painting a friend had painted, had been suspended inside the van near the roof. Using the screw holes from the garment holders above the windows on each side, I replaced them with eye hooks. I put eye hooks, to align with the ones in the van, on both sides of the wooden frame of the painting. Using wire Tom and I connected the eye hooks, raised the painting to the roof and secured it. It did not take up any usable space. There it was out of harms way. On top of the painting Tom placed his light weight paper posters so they would lay flat. We did this project well over a month before our departure. We wanted to make sure it would stay securely in place, it did.

The end of March Tom had completed his drivers training and took his road test shortly after his sixteenth birthday, which was March 28. He would be doing the driving on our move to Alaska.

Chapter 4

The day we were packed and ready to go, there wasn't any room left for the two lamp shades for our lamps we had packed to take along. So we placed them on our heads. Pictures were taken of us wearing these lamp shades. We had to leave the lamp shades behind, giving them to Cheryl. As we left we were deluged with cans of silly string being squirted at us. We left a tearful group of well-wishers behind us.

When we stopped in Alexandria for gas the station attendant/mechanic who had prepared the van for our journey, looked at our heavy load and warned us to be careful, we might break an axle. There was very little clearance between the tires and the van body. We were loaded with weight beyond a reasonable amount.

We left Alexandria June 7, 1993 two days after my graduation, and two years later to the day of our leaving for our vacation trip to Alaska in 1991. We never had any second thoughts about going to Alaska, this we were determined to do.

Our first day of traveling took us 378 miles from Alexandria, Minnesota. Much of this time we traveled in a windy heavy rain storm. Our first night brought us to a rest stop in North Dakota. We could not look for a camping place because of the storm. In our very crowded van we slept sitting up. We did not have to attempt to stretch out, lay down or turn, there wasn't any room to move in.

The floor space under my feet was full. A sack of potatoes shared my crowded foot space. I could not get both feet on the floor at the same time! I had to tilt myself sideways to get the van door shut.

Following an oil change in Montana we stopped in a town about 90 miles further down the road. There I noticed some oil on the ground. We went to a nearby station, there we were told that the man that changed the oil, put on the wrong filter. If this discovery had not been made the oil would have been lost resulting in major engine damage.

I am extremely afraid of snakes. One factor in making the decision to move to Alaska, Alaska does not have any snakes. In Montana we stopped at a rest stop to use the bathrooms. As I was getting out of the van, Tom pointed to a sign reading "Rattlesnakes have been seen in this area, please stay on Sidewalk." My trip to the bathroom waited until 30 miles, in the next town.

We stopped at a camp ground near the beautiful Columbia River in Washington State. I had been asking at camping places if there were snakes in the area. When I asked this question at the camp ground the man said, "Oh, if you go over there across the road in that dry area after dark, you can hear them rattle!!" He must have thought I was interested in snakes and was going to accommodate my interest. It was late and we were tired so we did camp there. The next morning I sent Tom out of the tent first to scout for snakes, there wasn't any.

In Canada it was rainy. When Tom turned on the windshield wipers the one on the drivers side went flying off, hanging by the washer hose. He tried to put it back on but to no avail. We stopped at "Smuzzams Cafe" and so-called station, near Yale, British Columbia. A man came out, may have been Smuzzam himself, he looked at the broken wiper and said, "Bad news, can't be fixed."

Attempting to travel further was futile. Returning to Smuzzams I called AAA, (CAA in Canada.) A tow truck was sent to tow us from Yale to Boston Bar. The tow truck driver thought he could fix the wiper with a piece of plastic from a bread bag! Well, even nonmechanical minded me knew that would not work, but I stood in the rain watching as he struggled to fix it.

Finally he decided to tow the van. Tom and I got into the tow truck, and put on our seat belts. The driver got into the truck, this man was really big. He held his seat belt in front of him because he needed to use two belts fixed together to fit around him, and I had his other one. He said, "Seat belt laws are strict in Canada."

Here we were in this truck with this guy holding the seat belt with one hand, driving with the other. He was towing our van with all our earthly possessions. Around and around up and down we went in the rain through the mountains as it was getting dark.

We arrived at Boston Bar and were told the station mechanic would be there the next morning. Now this was a comical sight--the tow truck driver unhooked our van, and we drove away. Usually if a car is being towed it is because it does not run. Ours ran fine, it just did not have a drivers-side windshield wiper.

We went to a hotel and got a room. Then went down to the cafe to eat. While we sat in a booth a young man, probably in this twenties or so, walked by us saying, "Hi." I replied, "Hi." On his way back by us he stopped and said to me, "I thought I knew you."

I quickly replied, "I don't think so!"

The next morning it was still raining. I went back to the service station, (with no place to sit), and I stood for an hour waiting for the mechanic. When he arrived I expected him to tell me the part would have to be ordered from Detroit, but first they would have to make it. Then it would have to shipped to a foreign country (Canada), which would take a year or so. But the guy quickly removed the unit from the passenger side and clipped it onto the drivers side!!! Why didn't one of those other knowledgeable fellows figure that out? We were not charged and went on our way. Thinking back we figured the clip was probably weakened during the wind storm in North Dakota.

We drove near Hope, British Columbia, where Rambo movies were filmed, in the steep mountain terrain. That was neat to see. Tom especially liked that because he had seen the Rambo movies and liked them.

We stopped at "The Store", somewhere in Canada. Steps led up either side of the door into the building. This wooden building was not any larger that a two-car garage. As I entered the building, I observed to my right, a counter, and to the left two racks of groceries. In the back was liquor sales. The clerk was waiting on a lady in the liquor department. He then came up to the front counter. I told him I wanted some stamps. He said, "Oh, the post office is back here."

I followed him to the back left corner. He went behind the official-looking postal window. I told him I wanted two US stamps. He needed to figure it out on an adding machine, not a calculator. He had an iron rod about 18 inches long, curved at one end with a round stamper on the end. With this he hit it on an ink pad, then slapped it down to cancel my stamped envelopes.

Adventures and excitement continued to follow us. On June 18, I told Tom I did not want to be on the road late, especially on Friday or Saturday nights. It was beginning to stay light longer, it was tempting to keep driving. We got a nice camp site. Tom was asleep, I was still awake, at 1:00 A.M., as

31

it was still very light out. I heard a screech, smashing noises and a girl screaming. I slept in a one-piece quilted jump-suit type outfit. It didn't really look like pajamas. I attempted to wake Tom, but he did not wake up. So, I quickly put on my shoes, not even grabbing my glasses, which I always wear. I unzipped the tent and ran to the camper next to us. Knocking on the door I asked the man who answered me if he had heard the crash? He said he had and was dressing. I asked what should we do? He said, "We had better go up there."

We ran through the wooded area, a short distance from the road, jumping over logs, stumps, and brush. When we got to the accident scene there was a very dirty man, partly from the dirt on the ground. People crawled out from under an overturned smashed pickup. A man had arrived ahead of us and jacked up the side of the pickup so the people could get out.

I walked up to one of the men and inquired about his condition, he was dazed and confused. Among other injuries his teeth were knocked out. About six feet or so from the wreck lay another man. Both men were about twenty years old. The one on the ground was badly injured. His teeth were knocked out, he was bleeding from his nose, mouth, and eyes. Walking around was a young teenage girl. She was complaining about her back hurting. We had problems keeping her in the area, she kept wondering off down the road.

There were five of us there to help. A couple from the camp ground and the man traveling on the road who stopped with the jack and the man and I from the camp ground all were helping. The couple brought blankets and pillows so we could try to keep the injured covered.

I checked the pickup for gasoline leaks, there were none. We were glad of that, we could stay in that area and not need to worry about moving the injured, in case of a fire. I attempted to calm the girl, but she was scared and upset.

A woman stopped, she had a CB but none of us knew the code for help and "Mayday," did not get a response. Someone did go for help to a small town several miles away.

When the sheriff arrived the girl became very upset, because they were three very drunk young people who did not want to see the law.

The man who had stopped to help said they had just passed him going at a very high speed when they lost control, rolled and crashed. We could not tell who the driver had been.

The ambulance arrived, the person injured the worst appeared to have internal injuries, broken pelvis, and undefined additional injuries, according to the ambulance crew.

I'll never know if they lived or not. Those in the accident probably don't remember the accident. But I am sure those of us who were there and helped will always remember the screams and chaos. There were beer cans scattered all over and the smell of alcohol was strong.

When the man and I walked back to our camp sites he told me he was a parole officer in Alberta, Canada and often dealt with the natives and their alcoholism problems.

The next morning I walked over to the camp next to us, saying to the man's wife, "I bet you would at least like to meet the woman who went running through the woods with your husband last night" She said, "Ya, and in your pajamas too, I heard!!"

About 800 miles before we got to the Alaskan border driving was very slow and difficult, through a long area of road construction. Our van was loaded down so that any bump, dip, or hole was major, even railroad crossings were difficult to handle. Tom needed to come to a complete stop many times before he could go ahead. Driving this part of the bad construction road we could only travel 20-25 miles per hour, seldom as fast as 35. We were traveling along at a snail's pace when, "PLOP" we sank into the mud. It was so deep we could not get out of the van. Tom put on the four-way flashers and we waited until a big road grader came and pulled us out. He did so, waving at us and we were on our way, we didn't even talk to him.

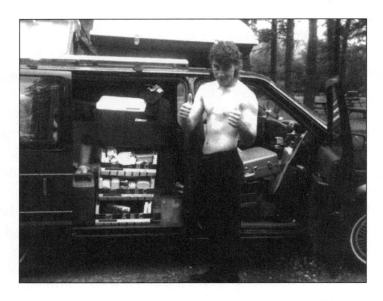

Tom on our way to Alaska, Yukon Territory, June 18, 1993

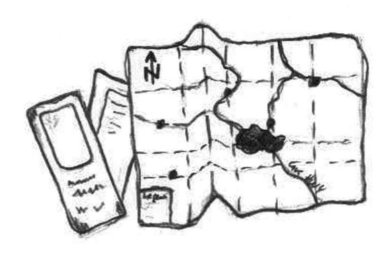

Chapter 5

Tom and I arrived in Fairbanks, Alaska the afternoon of June 20, 1993, Father's Day. We drove a short ways into the eastern part of town. Tom pulled the van into a parking lot of a closed pizza shop. We had gotten here, our destination, Fairbanks, Alaska, but we were at a loss as to where to go from there. The apartment on the university campus wouldn't be available until some time later in the summer. From where we had stopped we did not even know where the university campus was!

Searching through our booklets we found an advertisement for a bed and breakfast, we drove to it and rented a cabin. It was $40 for one night, too expensive for an extended length of time. From there we found a campground which was $15 a day, still to expensive.

After inquiring about camping places we were told that in North Pole there was a free campground. North Pole was about 11 miles from Fairbanks. We found the park in North Pole, it had pit toilets with a fence around the park. We parked outside the fence. We always activated our car alarm when we were away from it or sleeping, here we used it most of the time. Tom put up our sleeping tent then the screen tent over it and a picnic table, and we had a "home." We were quite comfortable, we played games, went for walks and once I went to a nearby shop and ordered a pizza to be delivered to our tent. I sure surprised Tom with that special treat.

People were friendly, several stopped to visit with us. I believe they were fascinated by our "home." One lady stopped to see if we needed any help. She visited us again later to check to see if we were okay or needed anything. Another lady invited us to her house for coffee.

We lived in the park for six days. We decided if we did not want to be a feature item in the local paper we had better find a "roof" home. One day while I was in the post office a reporter from the local paper approached me and asked, "What does the Fourth of July mean to you?" The next issue of the paper had my picture with my reply.

Finding an apartment was not easy, housing was scarce and expensive. While living in North Pole I went to the library nearly every day. I got a library card so Tom and I did quite a bit of reading. I read the local paper and made calls trying to find a place to live. One problem was, most rental places required first and last months' rent besides a hefty deposit along with a six month to a year lease. I was lucky to find a place that agreed to rent just as I needed, perhaps a month or so.

Our new home was a large one bedroom apartment. Tom made his room in the corner of the large living room. He liked that, that was where the free cable TV was. We had a dishwasher, but not many dishes to wash. The rent was $550 a month, including all the utilities and heat. It was hot so the heat wasn't needed. In mid July the temperature rose to above 90 F degrees a few times. It was in the 70's and 80's F most of the time we were in North Pole. The humidity was usually low, in the 20% range. The weather was beautiful, sometimes a slight breeze. We often went for walks and enjoyed sitting outside. We often had our door open, without a screen door, there weren't any bugs or mosquitoes.

When we moved into the apartment it took us an hour to unload the van, that did not include the two cargo carriers we had on top. We didn't have any beds or a couch. I had mentioned that to the caretaker when I paid the rent. When Tom and I returned from the local McDonalds for a bite to eat, we saw two men coming out of our apartment. I wondered what was going on. Then I saw the caretaker, they had put a bed and couch into our apartment. They told us is if there was anything else we needed, just let them know. We were pleasantly surprised.

We did not have any plates, we had been using the lids from two casserole dishes for plates. I decided to look for yard sales and try to find some plates. I asked a lady who was having a sale if she had any dinner plates for sale? She didn't, but another shopper came over to me and said she had some plates she would give me if I came over to her house and got them. Her name was Harriet Sewell and at her home I met her husband Jim. They invited me in for pie and coffee. I learned they had came to Alaska about 30 years ago from Brainard, Minnesota. Over the years we have kept in contact. Tom and I visited them a few times. And at home whenever we ate the plates reminded us of our new friends. Jim and Harriet also attended the same church in North Pole that I did, the short time I was there.

We had our days and nights turned around, easy to happen when it is always day-light during most of the summer. We decided we wanted to go to Denali Park and see Mt. McKinley. We got up at 3:00 A.M., even at that early hour it was quite light out. We drove 120 miles to the Park, taking a picnic lunch along, intended for noon. But we arrived at the Park at 6:00 A.M., at 8:00A.M. we ate our picnic, were back home by noon and went to sleep.

During our stay in North Pole the lady that had visited us in the park came and visited us in our apartment one day. She had seen me earlier and I told her we had found an apartment. She came and brought us two lovely plants. We lived in North Pole for a month. I was assured student housing at the university, but it became a waiting game. I called nearly everyday to check on our status. At last they told me that there were four apartments available at that time, seven people were on the list and we were last. I checked back in a few days and was told that three had taken apartments, three had withdrawn and we got the fourth.

We moved July 30, 1993 to a nice apartment on the university campus. Surprisingly it took more than one trip from North Pole to Fairbanks. We couldn't get it all back into the van! It was a furnished two bedroom apartment, with an arctic entry. I had heard people talk about arctic entries but didn't know what it was. It is a small entryway between the outside door and an interior door. This helps trap the cold air when one comes in from the outside. Nearly every house as well as public buildings have an arctic entry.

Chapter 6

We settled in our new apartment at Hess Village on the campus of the University of Alaska Fairbanks. Soon school started for Tom and me. New schools were a challenge for us. We did not know anyone in Fairbanks. We blindly plunged into the enrollment process, Tom in high school, me at the university. There was much to learn outside the classroom. Months before leaving Minnesota I had gotten most of my paper work done for school as well as a post office box, so some of the important things were done.

We knew the weather would be different than we were accustomed to. We didn't bring winter outerwear with us. I was fortunate to have a heavy parka given to me, which I still wear every winter. Tom had to walk 1/2 mile to school. He had a leather jacket that he wore everyday. I don't know how he managed to keep warm but he did, I believe he walked fast to keep warm. He wore shoe boots not snow boots. Often teens dress for appearance and not according to the weather. He has since learned the importance of proper winter dress in Alaska.

Our van also needed special heaters to keep it operable in cold weather. Before leaving Minnesota I had a head bolt heater, oil pan heater, and battery charger installed on the van. Every place where vehicles sit for any length of time there are electric outlets provided. If not, the owner will probably have to start their vehicle at different times during the time it sits to keep it in operable condition.

Houses and apartments all have electric outlets in the parking areas. Many have switches in the house or apartment for this plug in. We could plug in the van, go into the apartment and before going to bed turn the switch on. This was really handy, the switches saved an extra trip out into the cold, while saving on electricity.

Every once in a while out on the street we would see a car going down the street dragging a long electrical cord. The driver had neglected to unplug the car form the cord, therefore the driver was dragging it unsuspectingly along. This was always a comical sight.

All houses and apartments that are rentals, with water, included heat with the rent. This prevents water pipes from being frozen if the tenants do not pay their heating bill. If a tenant moved out unexpectedly the building would remain heated. This saves the landlord from the grief of broken water pipes.

Many homes in the Fairbanks area do not have wells. If they are beyond the city water system wells are often very expensive to have drilled, it is also hard to find water. Most cabins do not have water. Homes without wells have large storage tanks that hold a large amount of water. Water is delivered to the homes by water delivery trucks. This is on the same principle as oil delivery for heating. Many home owners haul their own water. There are special places where water can be purchased as well as some springs where people get their water.

When we first arrived in Fairbanks we were puzzled by

what the large plastic white tanks were for, that were in the back of many pickups. We later learned they were used for hauling water. The water is pumped into the tanks, then pumped into the holding tank in their house.

Of course homes without running water do not have indoor toilets, (except those with a chemical toilet system). The people have outhouses and take showers at a community shower facility, laundry is done at a laundromat. Houses with large holding tanks often have a complete plumbing system. This is accomplished with a pump that is installed to provide pressure in the pipes for water flow.

Living without running water is not a life-style that appeals to everyone. It takes getting use to and is a lot of extra work as well. Besides hauling water, gray water must be disposed of. However, there are many people who choose to live in cabins without running water and they get along quite well.

There are houses that have been built on ice lenses, which are layers of ice that when uncovered will melt away. Buildings on these are not stable and will often collapse. In Fairbanks there are areas where there is permafrost and when the tundra is moved it melts off causing unstable ground.

Tom and I lived in a cabin near Fairbanks for a short time during the summer of 1996. We hauled our water and had an outhouse. We did have heat, electricity, and telephone. Some cabins are quite rustic, without any utilities. There are trade-offs between living with all modern conveniences to a rustic life style. It is less expensive, often a secluded area, with low maintenance.

We became accustomed to our new life in Alaska. I eagerly attended my classes, I was enrolled in the education program, having completed my basic requirements in Minnesota. Among my array of classes I had an anthropology class. This class taught about the Alaskan Native People, mostly about the Athabaskan Indians and the Eskimos. In this class I became acquainted with several classmates who to this day have remained friends. This anthropology class ultimately had an indirect influence on my future. I will reveal that later in this book.

Life at the university went smoothly for us. We met new people and made friends, we also became acquainted with our neighbors, one neighbor, Shaun Lott has remained a close friend.

We were fascinated by the short daylight hours. It was odd to see car headlights on at 10:00 A.M. as well as 2:00 P.M. During the shortest days in the winter the sun just skirted the horizon. It remained low in the southern sky until it set. During the shortest time the sun rose at 10:59 A.M. and set at 2:41 P.M.. A big contrast to the long sun-up time in the summer. In Fairbanks during the longest days the sun rises at 1:59 A.M. setting at 11:48 P.M. But during that short period, it is still light. The daylight change is gradual, starting with about three minutes of change each day, working up to longer days in the summer increases of eight minutes or so each day. The same is in reverse for winter time.

Ice fog was another interesting phenomena. When the air is really cold, moisture accumulates in the air and ice crystals form, this is often extremely thick and creates low visibility. Ice fog is the heaviest in the downtown areas. It is increased with the exhaust from traffic. All vehicles must pass an emissions test to operate in Fairbanks. Local automobile service places do this test for a fee.

Fairbanks has very little wind at any time. In the winter this keeps the dense cold air from circulating, creating ice fog. The saying -- you can tell where the intersections are in Fairbanks, by the broken headlight and taillight glass on the street -- is quite true.

My neighbor and friend Shaun and I liked to go for walks, an inexpensive recreation besides excellent exercise. Our very favorite walks were late at night when it was really cold outside,

-30 degrees F or more. We enjoyed dressing in our parkas, warm mukluks, scarves and mittens. Our walks usually took us to a coffee shop, sometimes it was late and the coffee shop would be closed. But we enjoyed our walks anyway, being out for an hour or more at a time.

While I was a student at the university I did some of my training at an elementary school. I rode the bus to within about three quarters of a mile from the school, then walked the remaining distance. Mornings when the ice fog was really heavy I took a cab, mainly because I did not feel safe crossing at the busy intersections in the early morning. When I could not see any distance ahead of me I felt perhaps I was safer in a vehicle than on foot.

We were fascinated by the snow that piled high on fences and railings. Our patio had a wooden railing around it. When it snowed it remained on the railing and became quite high, two feet or so. Cars that were not driven during the winter would have very high piles of snow on top. Roofs that did not have enough slope needed to be cleared of the snow to prevent the roof from collapsing.

Often times we would hear people talking about going "outside." We would listen carefully, but it took some time before we realized that "outside" was a term for traveling, usually, to the lower forty eight states, Hawaii, or a different country. It is a term that neither Tom nor I have acquired. We are not comfortable with referring to traveling out of Alaska as going "outside." The word "outside" is often capitalized when written. We did not want to ask anyone what going "outside" meant, having been embarrassed when we asked what a snowmachine was. To us a snowmachine was a machine that made snow, such as the one at Spirit Mountain near Duluth, Minnesota. The snowmachine there makes snow for the ski slope. We couldn't imagine why Alaskans needed to make snow. We quickly learned that Alaskans call snowmobiles snowmachines. Any company that advertises these machines in newspapers or on TV refers to them as snowmobiles, when the advertisement comes from another state. Only Alaskans call them snowmachines.

We learned to wait and listen to find out what was meant by terms we were not familiar with. By the time spring arrived we began to hear another term "breakup." It didn't take us long to learn that that meant spring thaw. In Minnesota that time of the year was always called spring thaw. So our education outside of the classroom continued.

My anthropology class teacher told the class we could earn extra credit. I jumped at that chance. Extra credit is always helpful to boost a grade a little. There were several choices. One was to do volunteer work at the University Museum. I made the necessary contact to get started with my volunteer work. I worked a few hours a couple days a week. I placed pressed plants on pallets in the herbarium. It was interesting and I enjoyed the work. One day I asked the lady in charge if she knew where a teenage boy could get work for the summer? She told me she had a friend who owned Kantishna Roadhouse in a remote area in Denali National Park. It was located about 95 miles off the Parks Highway. If Tom was to work there he would need to stay there all summer. My first thoughts were -- I couldn't have him so far away for so long. I didn't say this, but told her I was interested in finding out more about it. She told me she would bring me an application for Tom.

When I told Tom about it I couldn't remember the name of the roadhouse. We didn't talk much about it, mainly because we didn't, know where or what it was. My next time at the museum I was given two applications for work at the roadhouse, one for each of us. We were excited as we pondered the idea of possibly working in a remote area of Alaska. Kantishna Roadhouse was located at the end of the road that goes into Denali National Park. We remembered hearing the name before. It was the place we couldn't go to on the Park bus we

44

were riding the summer of 1991.

I had a resumé made for Tom and me, I wanted our application to be the best possible. I turned in our applications to the lady at the museum. We later received a phone call and we set up a time for our interviews. The date was to be January 24, 1994.

Christmas break was nearly a month long for university students. I enjoyed this time to rest and unwind from all the fall activities that kept us busy, mainly school work. We didn't have a Christmas tree. We did have some lights and decorations that we brought with us. So we decorated our apartment to reflect the holiday season. It seemed odd to spend this time without the rest of the family. Phone calls to Minnesota did help bridge the gap. Our Christmas was quiet compared to previous ones, with just the two of us it was quite different.

Tom had acquired a morning paper route during his holiday break. A neighbor boy who had the route needed a substitute. He was going out of state for the holiday, his mom asked Tom if he would like to earn $40? When time and instructions were given Tom learned this was an early morning endeavor. It didn't sound so great, having to get up about 5:00 A.M. to get the papers all delivered before 7:00 A.M. Each morning when Tom returned home from the deliveries he would go back to bed. He did get $40, but has never forgotten how he messed up being able to sleep late during Christmas vacation.

Soon our vacation time was up, it was time to go back to school. As January ticked away we became more excited about our upcoming job interview. At last the day arrived. Tom and I got directions to the home of the roadhouse owner. We arrived on time and were greeted at the door by the owner and her assistant, we were invited in and offered refreshments.

During the interview we learned that the lodge owner's husband was also from Minnesota. She took us into the basement where he was making gold nugget jewelry to be sold at the roadhouse. We were impressed with the tiny figures and details he was working on.

We were told about the lodge, where and what it was. It sounded like an interesting place to work for the summer. Tom's duties would be dish washing, mine housekeeping. We were to check back in a few days to see if we were hired. A call back assured our being hired for the summer to work at Kantishna Roadhouse. To celebrate our good fortunate we went to our favorite Chinese restaurant. We were jubilant as we ate and discussed Kantishna. Neither of us could imagine what it would be like. We knew we would be entering this venture blindly, but our excitement and eagerness over-rode any apprehension we had.

We finished up our school year and prepared to go to our summer jobs. To avoid paying rent on our apartment while we were gone we rented a storage unit for our belongings. During the summer the university rented our apartment to summer students. We were assured we would get it back again in the fall.

Author on the way to school, January 31, 1994

Chapter 7

We decided to trade our van in for a different car. It had been faithful to us for several years, it was time for a change. I could walk to all my classes in less than ten minutes so I didn't really need a car for just myself.

Tom had received an inheritance from his dad. He wanted to get his own, first car. We went car shopping, he found the one he wanted, it was a little red Buick Sky Hawk. The dealer took him for a test ride, it was just what he wanted. With the van trade-in and his money he bought the car. With Tom in the driver's seat we started for home, well sort of. He had not driven a stick shift before, neither had I. He proceeded by pushing in the clutch and break, shifted to an ahead gear then took both feet off the pedals. We lunged forward and stalled. This procedure was continued for over an hour as we lurched our way toward home.

It was about 5:00 P.M. on a Friday in May the traffic was at its peak. We were not looked upon as being among friendly souls. Our lurching and stalling at intersections was less than desirable. By the time we had gotten very far we were overcome with laughter, while other drivers failed to see the humor. When we finally arrived back to our parking lot we stopped and let out a big sigh. We were thankful to be back home safe and secure.

Our next priority was for Tom to learn how to drive his new chariot. The experience we had just had was one we did not want to repeat. I promptly went to a neighbor, he opened the door to my knock. Trying to restrain the panic in my voice I said, "Gilbert, will you please do me a favor, could you teach my kid how to drive a stick shift?"

I then related our experience to him. With a big smile he said, "Sure."

Tom and Gilbert returned sometime later. Now Tom wore a big smile. He was pleased that now he could drive his car without enduring embarrassment, thanks to our kind neighbor Gilbert Campbell.

Chapter 8

May 4, Tom returned home from school excited to tell me something. He said, "Mom I have something to show you." He got the video camera and hooked it up to the TV and proceeded to show me a video of a cow moose and two calves. In the morning he opened the door to go to school. But he could not get out of the house, because the three moose were by the door. He then closed the door and got the video camera to take a picture. I had missed seeing them at that time because I was still in bed. We saw these moose at different times during that month and again in the fall.

Our first school year in Alaska ended in May 1994. We were looking forward to our summer employment. With the car packed, our belongings in storage, and directions to Kantishna, we headed out of town. The drive down the Parks Highway was beautiful. Spring had emerged from the long cold winter. With new leaves and green grass, there was barely a hint of winter passed. In Alaska May is a beautiful month. Winter is sent away for a few months. The snow had given way to green grass, trees, shrubs, and beautiful wild flowers. During the summer wild flowers and grasses grow fast to get their growing done in a short time.

Out trip into the Park began with a fifteen mile drive to the check point, at Savage River. Here we displayed our pass, then were on our way. It would be nearly four hours before we reached Kantishna Roadhouse, another 80 miles beyond the check point. The road was narrow, crooked as well as unfamiliar to us. We were instructed to drive very slow. Speed laws were enforced on that road. Much of the time we were not able to even travel more that thirty miles per hour. As we proceeded we saw remnants of winter, in the higher elevations there was snow along side the road.

Upon arrival at Kantishna Roadhouse we were greeted by workers who had arrived ahead of us. Within a few days the entire staff was on hand. Some were returning employees, others, like us, new employees most were from states other than Alaska seeking an Alaskan adventure.

We settled in and began to learn our duties, Tom was a dishwasher, I was a housekeeper, cleaning rooms, cabins, and doing laundry for the lodge. This was a new experience for us. Neither of us had ever worked at a lodge in a remote setting. The area was beautiful with mountains all around and a creek nearby.

We had a room in employee housing, a new building with small but adequate rooms. Tom spent one night in the loft of our room and decided he would rather have a wall tent. The loft was too small and not to his liking. The wall tent was a canvas stretched around a wooden frame creating an enclosure suitable to live in. There he spent the rest of the summer and was quite comfortable, I then had the room to myself.

My supervisor, Leann Kowalke was excellent at training, I quickly learned what was required of me. I enjoyed my work although it was hard physical labor. There were twenty-nine rooms and cabins to be cleaned. This was done by three housekeepers, two at a time rotating for days off, we also did the laundry.

Most of the time the rooms had guests, they were there one or two nights leaving on the 7:00 A.M. Kantishna Roadhouse bus. People came from all over the world. All were eager to see and learn about the enchanting state of Alaska. When I was asked questions about Alaska I often thought back three short years, when I was a visitor, some of the same questions posed to me I had also asked. People hunger to learn all they can when they are here. Usually their visit is only a few days or a couple weeks or so, hardly long enough to comprehend the vastness of the state, along with all its beauty and wonder. Many visitors expect to see wild animals in a zoo-like setting. There are thousands of wild animals in Alaska spread out over millions and millions of acres. It often takes time and patience to see these animals, but it is always worthwhile.

We also learned about Kantishna Roadhouse. It had a new addition put on the year before. Some of the workers were talking about Jerome building the new log part of the lodge. I asked, "Who is Jerome?" I was told he was the owner's husband's brother, I had never seen Jerome. I was impressed with the beautiful lodge building that he had done the log work on.

Everything was going smoothly at the lodge. We both made new friends and enjoyed our new experience. The work kept us busy. I had brought along my school books for the upcoming school year. I read them during the summer, this helped me get a little head start on my subjects.

On July 7, in the afternoon a couple of the guys from the maintenance department were doing some yard work. They needed some help in moving a heavy rock. Tom was asked to come out from the kitchen and help. Tom and Clayton Flagg, lifted the rock, about 300 pounds, into a wheelbarrow. The rock shifted, tipped the wheelbarrow and fell onto the ground. They once again picked it up and placed it back into the wheelbarrow. This time Tom did not get his hand out in time, the rock smashed the side of his hand, quite bad, breaking open the skin. He went into the lobby of the lodge seeking help for his injury. He was holding his injured hand cupped in the other hand up in front of him. That position must have appeared like he was holding something, a guest came up to him and inquired, "Oh what little animal do you have there?"

Help was quickly found for his injury and it was cleaned and bandaged. It was to late to go to the clinic in Healy, over 100 miles away, that would have to wait until the next day. The next day work schedules were shuffled so Tom and I could go to the clinic in Healy, that was an all day trip, there and back.

Tom's hand healed nicely, but he could no longer be a dishwasher a replacement was found, Tom was placed in housekeeping with me. He quickly adjusted to his new routine and fit in quit well. He wasn't all that thrilled about making beds and cleaning bathrooms, but he did. Tom had his eye on the maintenance department. There were thirty-three employees at the lodge with several guys in the maintenance department. He thought he would like to work there, they did cool things! He was happy when he was transferred to the "guys" department.

One evening I went to eat supper, sat down and looked at the end of the dining room where the mail holder for employees was. I saw a large brown envelope sticking up higher than the rest. I could see the very large printing in the corner -- "ENCLOSED: MEMBERSHIP FOR FAIRBANKS NUDIST SOCIETY." I jumped up, knowing it was addressed to me, and said, "I'll get her!!!" I even knew who it was from without reading any further. I took the envelope, sure enough addressed to me, opened it and inside was a letter from Shaun and a Fairbanks newspaper (we seldom got a newspaper at the lodge so Shaun had sent me one). But, she had to play a trick on me in the process. She knew several people would see the mail before I would get it.

I later talked to Bruce Burnell, who was the bus driver that brought the mail that day. He said he saw it when he got the mail and made sure it was address down where he had the mail, the entire six hour drive from the park entrance. He had a bus load of tourists and he didn't want anyone to see the envelope!

Tom and I got to do some pretty exciting things. We went on a flight seeing trip near Mt. McKinley with Greg LaHaie of LaHaie Air, as pilot. We saw some glaciers besides the fantastic view from up above. I got to go canoeing in Wonder Lake. It was calm and a beautiful evening, my friends Leann and her fiancé Richard Clawson took me in their canoe we had a spectacular view of Mt. McKinley. Tom and I along with co-workers/friends went to a very remote cabin. Clayton drove Bruce and Bonni Burnell, Tom and I part way to the Parker Cabin. We then hiked about three hours across the river and through brush. Each of us carried our own packs with clothes and personal items as well as carrying our sleeping bags, food and supplies. Our loads were heavy.

When we got to the cabin we were hungry and tired. First the boards had to be taken off the windows. The boards were there to prevent bears from breaking into the cabin. On the boards were nails driven so the pointed edge was out, this discouraged bears from trying to get in. In front of each window hung a tin can on a string, this was also a bear deterrent. Bruce and Tom took the boards down letting light and fresh air into the cabin.

The cabin was furnished with a table, beds, stove, cooking supplies, odds and ends. In the cold storage hole, a covered hole in the kitchen area, there was flour and rice. Bruce and Tom went to a nearby spring to get water. They then built a fire on which steaks and potatoes were cooked. We had a delicious meal. While Bonni and I cleaned up Bruce and Tom made a cribbage board by carving it out of wood, they made it to be left at the cabin.

After cleaning up we decided to go for a walk, exploring around. Bruce and Bonni had brought along one of their dogs from their dog sled team. We all set out on our walk. The guys had some string which they attempted to make fishing poles with sticks, it wasn't too successful, but they had fun anyway.

As we walked along we heard a loud commotion in nearby tall grass. It was quickly brought to our attention that Maggie, the sled dog, had just been introduced to Mr. Porcupine. With the howling, hurting dog we headed back to the cabin. A couple of hours were spent in an attempt to remove the numerous quills Maggie had protruding from her mouth and nose. Maggie protested fearfully so the quill removal attempt was abandoned. Bruce and Bonni decided they needed to get the dog to Fairbanks to the veterinarian. They set out about 11:00 P.M. walking back to Kantishna.

Tom and I were suddenly alone without protection, not knowing exactly what to do. My concern was bears, we put the boards back over the windows. Inside the cabin was total darkness. Tom lighted a lamp which quickly lit up the cabin. I wrote in the journal that was there. Others previously had written in it, so it was interesting to read of the experiences others had had. We retired for the night, wondering what the next day would bring. We slept late the next morning with the darkness inside the cabin we were unable to see what time it was.

A pick up time had been agreed upon before we left Kantishna. Clayton was to meet us at the place he had left us the day before. This time was set for 12:00 noon, we hurried to get our things together. Tom had taken a board off one window for light when we first got up. The view out that window was spectacular. Mt. McKinley was framed in this window creating a splendid view.

Loaded down with our gear, we struck out to meet our ride. We chose a different route back. There was an old trail that crossed Moose Creek several times, it was also shorter that the previous route we had taken. I wanted to keep track of the number of times we waded across the river. I asked Tom what would be a good way to keep track? He said, "Each time we get across the river put a small stone in your pocket, and when we are done crossing the creek count the stones."

That was a good idea, I counted the stones in my pocket, I had eleven. I still have those small stones to remind me of our difficult trudge back.

Along the way we saw fresh bear tracks as well as bear droppings. A bear was not far from us, but we did not know where it was. Later we surmised the bear had picked up the scent of the blood from the injured dog, in the wee hours of the night it had perhaps been near Bruce, Bonni, and their dog.

Clayton picked us up as scheduled; the end of that adventure, it was now time to go back to work. The dog was taken to Fairbanks and successfully treated.

Late in the summer, I heard my co-workers talk about picking blueberries. This I wanted to know more about, I really like blueberries. I was told where to go to pick the berries. Obtaining a container from the lodge I set out to pick berries. After a short time I returned to the lodge and announced to my fellow workers, as I walked by a group of them sitting by a picnic table, "Where are the blueberries? I only found these awful sour berries which I do not like." I was informed that those were blueberries, well I begged to differ, those were not blueberries! I quickly learned that Alaska blueberries are not anywhere near like the sweet flavorful blueberries I had become accustomed to in Minnesota. Alaska blueberries are more like a huckleberry, no likeness to the blueberry of the lower states, except for the color. I have seen acres and acres, as far as I could see blue with these berries and thought how great it would be if they were good. Many people, however, like these blueberries and will go a great distance to pick them. I have attempted to eat pie and jelly/jam made from these berries, but did not care for them. I did use some of the syrup-like liquid that we received as a gift on ice cream, the ice cream mellowed out the tartness.

Soon the summer came to an end. We had made new friends, some we continued to keep in contact with. One such friend is Celeste Rak from Chicago, who was a guest at the Kantishna Roadhouse during that summer. We have continued to exchange letters, cards, and pictures. Frank and Tex Brochu, co-workers of mine, have remained friends. They live in Canada. I did get a letter from Erika Rothenbuhler who had gone back to Switzerland. Regretfully, I did not write back to her. From time to time I ran across her letter and thought I should write, but didn't. On occasion, while in Fairbanks, I will see someone I worked with at Kantishna.

Tom and I said our good byes and returned to Fairbanks. It was now August, snow would soon be blanketing this wonderland, the land would now lay in wait until next season. People would come again to enjoy the wonders of Denali National Park.

We moved back into our apartment on the university campus. School routine was easier that second year. Being familiar with the campus and procedures made things go smoothly. Meeting new people was easy in the classroom, one such friend and former classmate as well as a neighbor was Al and Maggie Wasuli. They lived in the village of Kotlik on Norton Sound, on the west coast of Alaska.

Kantishna Roadhouse, summer 1994
(photo taken by Allen Prier)

Tom and Bruce making cribbage board,
July 3, 1994

Parker cabin, July 3, 1994

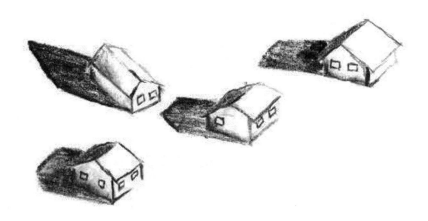

Chapter 9

During spring break, March 13 through March 17, Tom and I went to Kotlik to visit the Wasuli family. It was exciting when Maggie invited us, neither of us had ever been to an Eskimo village. Our plans were filled with excitement as once again we were going to explore the unknown.

Tom and I had met Jim and Robin Barker, friends of Maggie and Al. The Barkers knew some people in Bethel, Alaska who had a bed and breakfast. We needed a place to stay one night on our way to and from Kotlik. I flew from Fairbanks to Anchorage then Bethel in one day, staying in Bethel overnight. Tom and I could not leave Fairbanks on the same day, because of the limited space on the small plane between Bethel and Kotlik, I left a day ahead of Tom.

Paul Longpre met me at the airport in Bethel. This village was on the Kuskokwim River, without trees or mountains, the area is quite flat. I stayed at the comfortable bed and breakfast, until departing time, the next morning. Paul took me back to

58

the airport. I boarded a small plane for my flight to Kotlik. The plane made several stops at small village air strips. Besides mail and luggage the plane carried only three passengers. As I was riding in this small aircraft I noticed the amount of Duct Tape that was inside the plane, holding various things up and together. Duct Tape does hold life together, in this case literally!! I also observed several areas around the doors in which I could see light between the door and plane body.

I was dressed in my heavy parka, layers of pants, mittens, and boots. Even with all my heavy winter gear I became very cold. I asked the pilot if there was a problem with the heater? He told me, "When it is this cold the heater doesn't do any good". I don't believe I have ever before or since been so cold.

Al met me at the airstrip, there was not an airport there, just a very small three-sided structure at the airstrip. Al came on his snowmobile to pick me up. There were no roads, cars, or trucks in Kotlik. This too was a village without trees, some shrubs and low bushes, the area was flat without mountains. Maggie had commented on how they don't like it where there are trees; "it makes us feel hemmed in, we prefer the open landscape." All travel is done in the winter by snowmobile, dog sled, or walking. In the summer four-wheelers are used. The Wasuli home was across the river from where the plane had landed. I was quickly welcomed into the house by Maggie, their home was warm and cheerful, it was great to be inside and I finally got warm.

Young Chris Wasuli was at home and excited to see us again. Soon his sisters Helen and Kathy came home from high school. We all joined in lively conversation, catching up on all the events of our lives, worlds apart.

The next day Tom arrived at the airstrip, he too was welcomed. Chris was especially excited to see Tom, he had visited us when they lived in Fairbanks and really liked Tom, a big boy he could look up to. Tom had stayed in Bethel too, enjoying the nice bed and breakfast.

The first thing Tom said when he came into the house was, "Where are all the cars?" He was astonished by the small village without cars. We all had a good laugh and explained to him that there were not any cars in Kotlik.

We had much to learn and quickly did so in the short week we were in Kotlik, an Yupik Eskimo village. The Eskimo population borders the coastal areas of Alaska and most of the Indian population are in the interior. Many of the residents spoke Yupik, some did not speak English. Along with Maggie, I visited some of her relatives and friends. Wherever I went, I was welcomed and enjoyed the visit. One of Maggie's sisters gave me a sewing kit that she had made, I was honored to receive the gift. In some homes we visited, I could not take part in the conversation, but was fascinated to listen to their lively Yupik language. Most places we were offered refreshments. Maggie and I spent a couple of afternoons and evenings visiting. Maggie also took me ice fishing on the Yukon River. We didn't catch any fish but it was fun trying. Being my first visit to an Eskimo village it was interesting to observe their unique culture. I had learned a little about the Native people of Alaska, but that came no way near to actually being there. Their way of life, in many ways, did not resemble society as I was accustom to.

Most houses were similar in size, all one story, rambler-type, built on permafrost. Because of the permafrost basements and wells are not dug. The water supply came from the Yukon River. Bleach, in small amounts, added to the water purified it. Instead of outhouses or traditional bathrooms, honey buckets were used for toilets. These were placed out in front of the homes when they became full, to be picked up and disposed of such as a garbage pick up route. Showers and laundry facilities were in the community center, which were provided for a fee.

Some people had saunas. This was another new experience for me, I went with several other women in Wausli's sauna. Since high school gym class I had not been bathing in the nude with other people, I hoped my reluctance did not show. I quickly found that I could not tolerate the high heat of the sauna, as the others could. Most of my time was spent in an outer room wrapped in a towel! Since that time in the sauna I had a chance to take another sauna, at a friends place near Fairbanks, in which I was better able to tolerate the heat.

Kotlik had schools and churches as well as two stores. The store in which Tom and I went with Maggie, carried items from toothbrushes, shirts, mittens, meat, canned and fresh food as well as towels and paper items. It was a general store with a wide variety. Prices were quite a bit higher there, especially fresh produce. Fresh foods are difficult to get. Freezing is a problem in the winter when food must come from far away.

We attended the Catholic church on Sunday morning. The service was all in Yupik with English booklets to follow along. After the service we met many people as we enjoyed coffee, doughnuts, and conversation.

Delicious meals, made by Maggie, graced the Wausli's table. The Eskimos are accustomed to eating seal oil with their meals. I asked if I could taste some. Al recommended that I didn't taste it, assuring me that it was pretty strong in flavor.

One evening Al's brother Robert, from the village of Emmonak, came to have Al give him a hair cut. He was a small man about sixty-five years old and very spry. He had arrived on his snowmobile. Al took a large black plastic garbage bag, cut a hole in the bottom end, then placed it over Robert's head onto his shoulders to keep the hair from falling all over him. I thought that was a clever way to keep the hair off of the clothes of the one getting the hair cut.

Al carved a beautiful wooden bowl and ladle out of driftwood that he had picked up along the shore. I will always treasure this special gift made by my friend in Kotlik.

We were invited to attend a potlatch in Stebbins, but we had to leave the day before it was to take place. Tom and I were sad when the time came for us to depart. We had a most memorable time in this Yupik Eskimo village. We knew we could not return anytime soon, if ever. We were invited to come back as well to visit them at their summer fish camp. We saw pictures of their fish camp and I sure would like to go there, maybe someday.

Again, we had to travel apart to Bethel, I left first, Tom later the same day. We met back at the bed and breakfast in Bethel. From there, the next day, we flew together back to Anchorage then Fairbanks. That memorable trip will always remain to be one of our highlights of Alaskan adventures. Distance keeps us from seeing each other, but Maggie and I keep in contact with letters, pictures, and phone calls. I remain hopeful that some day I will be able to visit them again, perhaps at their fish camp.

Village of Kotlik, Northon Sound, Alaska, March 13, 1995

Headstart building, Kotlik,
March 14, 1995

Tom in front of Kotlik Store,
March 14, 1995

Al and Tom, Kotlik, March 15, 1995

Maggie by her childhood home,
Kotlik, March 14, 1995

63

Chapter 10

With the ending of spring break it was back to school for us. It didn't seem like spring, however, there was still plenty of deep snow around.

Tom had some exciting events in his life. He was asked to design a tee-shirt for Kantishna Roadhouse to be sold the next season in the gift shop. His artistic ability had always been apparent, even as a young boy his drawings were excellent. The design was to advertise the Kantishna Roadhouse bar, Smoky Joe's Salon. The design was to be a picture of the bar with gold miners standing at the bar. The miners were to appear as ghosts, being able to see detail through them as they stood at the bar. Tom was given a picture of some old gold miners, one I remember being Joe Quigley, who died in 1958. Along with three other long-dead gold miners Tom drew them to appear as though they were standing by the bar with drinks in hand. Above the bar was a picture of Smoky, the dog the bar was named after. Tom put this together to create a great design for the shirt. Under the picture was the inscription "Serving fine Alaskan Spirits," a clever caption for the picture.

West Valley High School, where Tom attended school, also recognized his artistic ability. He was chosen as a possibility of being one of fourteen students to go to Russia. This was a cultural exchange for young people to learn about another country. It was the *Russian-American School Linkages Program.* The following is a quote from the project profile in the *Russian-American School Linkages Program Handbook for U.S. Escorts in Russia* (no page number).

The overall goal of the proposed program is to enhance the existing linkages between U.S. and Russian secondary vocational schools through increased exchanges of students, teachers, and administrators. The Center on Education and Training for Employment at The Ohio State University.......

The Russian-American Exchange Program will begin with the 1994 fall academic semester and conclude during summer 1995. A total of 14 U.S. and Russian secondary vocational schools will participate in an exchange network in which they will be paired for *both student and teacher/administrator exchanges.* It is anticipated that a total of 196 secondary students and 42 teacher/administrators (14 students, 2 teachers, and 1 administrator from each of the 14 schools) will be exchanged during the 1994-95 academic school year.

The length of the student and teacher/administrator exchange programs will be 4 weeks. U.S. locations for the program include Plain City, Ohio; Ashland, Ohio; Hamilton, Ohio; Fairbanks, Alaska; Billings, Montana; Canadian Valley, Oklahoma; and Clayton, Ohio. Russia locations include Tomsk, Barnaul, Yakutsk, Kemerovo, Krasnoyarsk, Omsk, and Khabarovsk....

We attended meetings at the school to learn more about the upcoming trip. Tom was included to be among the group to go to Russia and Siberia in April. There were more meetings to get all the particulars in place. Much work, time, and effort went into this project, by the staff at West Valley as well as the Hutchison Career Center.

Prior to the Alaskan students' trip to Russia and Siberia, students from Kemerovo, Siberia would be coming to Fairbanks and stay with host families. When possible these students would stay with those who in turn would stay with them in Kemerovo.

Olga Kostuk, age 16, would be coming to our home for a nearly two week stay. The day of the Russians arrival was to be March 28, 1995, Tom's eighteenth birthday. The day arrived, the excitement of the new arrivals overshadowed Tom's birthday, even though it was his eighteenth, a milepost for a teenager.

Olga was welcomed into our home. Tom and I had divided my bedroom in half and added a bed for her. We hoped she would be comfortable in her area, however it was quite small.

Language was a barrier between the Russian and American students. Some of the students did quite well with English. Olga had a Russian-to-English book to refer to in order to improve communication. There were many times when we all struggled to understand one another. Food was one of the biggest adjustments Olga faced in our home. She did not know what many things were. She was willing to try new foods as well as some other new experiences.

My friend Roni Pruett took Tom, me, and Olga's friend Irina for a balloon ride above Fairbanks. The view was spectacular up there. A clear calm day made for a most enjoyable ride. Olga, however, would not go up in the balloon.

Olga missed her best friend Irina who was in a different host home. Between the two girls they somehow arranged for Irina to come to our house. She spent the last part of their stay in our home, now we had two girls that we could not always understand. However, Irina's English was quite a bit better than Olga's.

They attended school each day with Tom. Getting acquainted with the girls was a small step toward learning what Tom would expect when he would travel to their land.

The girls did their laundry by hand, saying machine clothes washing was the "lazy way." Jeans were washed in the bath tub and wrung out by hand, then hung to dry. After they left, I was putting my things back into a chest of drawers they had used, I found a pair of underwear. One of the girls had laid it flat in the bottom of a drawer to dry and forgot it. I surmised they did not want anyone to see their underwear so they hid them in an empty closed drawer after laundering them.

Among the gifts they left for me were, small birch bark carved baskets, a beautiful colorful scarf, linen table cloth, jewelry and trinket items. Some they gave to me outright others they left for me to find, sometimes in a conspicuous place, other times not. Notes would usually accompany these gifts thanking me for having them there or just a--here's a gift--note. The time spent with the girls was interesting and rewarding.

It was mid-April when the girls returned home, preparations began in full swing for the Alaskan students' trip. Medical exams as well as inoculations required for foreign travel were part of the preparation. A list of what was necessary to take along was carefully checked and purchased.

Time to the big day passed quickly, the day to leave for Russia. With all in order the students along with school staff boarded their plane. I had written a letter to make a special request. Tom and I agreed if something should happen to me while he was gone he was not to be notified. Most parents, students, and chaperons had set up a method of keeping in touch during the trip. Tom could not do anything to change any unfortunate event that might happen to me. I did not want anything to interrupt and spoil his, perhaps, once in a lifetime trip.

I met slight objection to my request, but this was our decision, so it was honored. Fortunately nothing happened. I missed Tom and waited anxiously for his return, at the same time hoping he was having the time of his life. His words, later, when he got home were, "Ya, it was pretty cool."

The day they left they were in the air some place between California and New York at the time of the Oklahoma City Bombing. Tom said they were not told about it right away. Some of the first accounts of it, through foreign messages, were completely false. Information filtering from foreign sources were greatly distorted.

I was excited and tearful when I met Tom at the airport in Fairbanks, after all, this was the first time we had been apart for that length of time and so far away.

He had many experiences that he will always remember and some he will treasure. One experience that he had was that he broke out with some type of rash. The host family and others pampered and fussed over him. He was taken to the emergency room of a hospital. He said he watched them really close, not knowing what they might do. He said a nurse had her apron held together with a hypodermic needle. They told him, through translator, that they were going to give him an IV containing charcoal to remove the poison or what ever was causing his rash. Tom said he watched and made sure the nurse used a new needle (one in a wrapper). I am not sure I would have let them do this to me.

After Tom returned home I called the clinic to explain the rash and where Tom had been. The clinic instructed us to use the back door and not go into the waiting room, we were treated as though we had the plague. When I told the doctor Tom had been treated with charcoal IV he reacted in a negative manner, stating that that was an unwise idea. The doctor did not know what was causing the rash, therefore no treatment. Later that week we saw on a news program on TV that charcoal is a treatment for removing poisons from the body. I guess the

Russians knew what they were doing. The rash disappeared and did not return.

The night Tom arrived back home he had many things to tell and show me. He quickly unpacked, bringing out all the interesting things he had gotten in Russia. We talked and look at things until the wee hours of the morning. He had many stories to tell me. It had been a journey he would never forget. His biggest impression was how lucky we Americans are. He said those people have so little, they live mostly drab lives. He did say however, that the people were warm and friendly toward them. Tom, being eighteen was allowed to drive his host family car. He expressed that was quite an experience.

He did not stay with either of the two girls' families who had been here. He did not get to visit Olga's family. He said he thought perhaps they were very poor and did not want him to see where they lived.

Unfortunately we did not keep in touch through letters. I still have addresses and hope sometime I will get around to writing to Olga or Tom's host family.

Chapter 11

Summer was rapidly approaching. It was time to prepare for our return to Kantishna. This time we did not put our belongs in storage, but retained our apartment. We had a better idea as to what to take along, being our second summer at the lodge. We rode one of the Kantishna buses to the lodge, leaving Tom's car in Fairbanks. It was the end of May when we arrived at Kantishna. Tom was in the maintenance department and I was supervisor of housekeeping. I got my same room back and Tom got a room, in the same building, to himself. There were new employees as well as returning ones. It was interesting to see who would be returning from the previous summer. In my department all were new except me.

That summer, like the previous one, proved to be busy. The guest rooms were occupied most of the time. Tom built a serving table for the lodge. One of his primary duties was to wash the Kantishna buses each day. Tom and Clayton painted the fuel barrels black and white "Holstein" design. These tanks were in the back near the generator building, not in direct view for guests. They were a comical sight when all painted.

The tee-shirts, Tom designed, were a good selling item in the lodge gift shop. I was proud to see his art work displayed and for sale. He too, was pleased, although he didn't reveal it. He has always been quiet and shy, but I knew he was pleased.

That was our last summer at Kantishna, the lodge was sold to Doyon, a native corporation. We did not plan on returning there to work. We would check during the winter at other places for work next summer.

Tom Schleicher with tee-shirt he designed
for Kantishna Roadhouse, July 8, 1995

Chapter 12

When we visited Minnesota during the Christmas holiday in 1994, my oldest daughter, Cheryl Patterson, and I discussed the possibility of my twelve-year-old grandson Tim, visiting us in Alaska. He was really excited at the possibility of living in Alaska with us for a year. Much had to be done and planned for Tim to go to Alaska. When Tom and I returned to Alaska we began making plans and room for him.

Grandson Tim Patterson, arrived in Fairbanks August 13, 1995. At last the big day had arrived. All the planning and anticipation had unfolded. Thirteen-year-old Tim, arrived on a beautiful August day. His face revealed the excitement and perhaps slight apprehension he was feeling. Conversation soon revealed he was happy to finally arrive in Alaska. Months of planning had made his dream a reality.

Tim had only one short night of rest before we plunged him into a whirl of activities. Tom and I had planned a camping trip that would last nearly two weeks. The day previous to Tim's arrival, a friend had given me a beautiful bouquet of roses. She did not know I had planned on not being at home to care for the flowers. I pondered the problem and decided to take the flowers with me on our camping trip. That wasn't a decision the boys shared with me, however.

Tom traded his little red car for a Toyota pickup, the day before Tim arrived. With the pickup packed with food, camping gear, and oh yes, the flowers, we headed down the Richardson Highway. Copper Center was our first camping site. Nearly mid-August was bringing cooler air temperatures, cooler temperatures assured us more plentiful camping areas.

Our travels took us to Valdez, we wanted to show Tim the ocean. While there we found the fishing boat we had gone on in 1991 when Sandy caught the 72 pound halibut. The owner was not around so we left a note on it to tell him who had stopped in to visit.

After leaving Valdez we went to the Matanuska Glacier, between Glennallen and Palmer. There we camped in the same place we had four years previously. The glacier had changed a lot with the movement it makes slowly over the years. It was interesting to see the change it had made. We did some hiking on the glacier, Tim got his feet stuck in the glacier silt and lost his shoes in the mud as he attempted to pull his feet out. Tom retrieved his shoes, but Tim had some pretty mud-laden shoes that took quite some time to dry, they resembled blocks of concrete. After our adventure there, we headed toward Palmer then to Anchorage.

Oh yes, each night we camped, the bouquet of flowers were taken from the pickup and placed on a picnic table. I endured sputtering and grumbling from the boys about my flowers. They weren't in complete agreement with me, that the flowers looked very nice on the picnic table! I believe it had something to do with the sight of these bright flowers displayed on a picnic table in a campground. They viewed it as being "out of place," and they wondered what other people might think when they saw campers with a vase of flowers on their picnic table?

73

Not only their presence, but the inconvenience, of these flowers were met with less than enthusiasm. After all, camping, they thought, was mostly a guy thing. So why did they have to deal with a vase of flowers; keeping them from getting damaged, tipping over, while traveling, keep water in the vase, and worst of all being seen with them? Why did they have to endure such humiliation, these teen-age boys?

They probably never understood why these flowers needed to go camping anyway. But, they did and, all involved survived. It was a glorious occasion for them, the day they could finally toss the withered, much dried, hardly recognizable former bouquet over an embankment. Great cheers of joy rang through the air as the dead flowers disappeared over the edge. I believe those two boys will always see a vase of flowers in a different light than most people.

On our agenda was an overnight stay at Kantishna, as guests. There were still workers there so Tim got to see where Tom and I had worked. We headed home, our trip quickly came to an end. We had had a good trip, were tired and anxious to get home. We had taken quite a few pictures and wanted to get them developed. When we got our pictures developed, lo and behold those flowers once again appeared, in pictures to be preserved forever!

Tim had never been on a train, so I had planned a train trip for him. We took a shuttle bus from Fairbanks to Denali National Park. Tim and I spent the entire day in the park entrance area, checking out gift stores and all the attractions. One of the hotels was celebrating Christmas on August 25, 1995, the day we were there. During the winter this part of the park, hotels, shops, attractions, and venders are all closed, Christmas is celebrated in August instead of December. After a day at the park we boarded the Alaskan Railroad Passenger Train, going back to Fairbanks. We enjoyed the unique experience of having a meal in the train's diner car. Tim was thrilled with the train ride.

Getting back to Fairbanks meant school was imminent, for the three of us. Of course there was many new things about Alaska Tim was learning. Even attending school was quite different from his school in Minnesota. He met every challenge with enthusiasm and eager to do and learn more.

October 5, 1995 will be a day Tim and I will always remember. In the early evening Fairbanks had a 6.2 earthquake. Tim was upstairs, I yelled for him to come down and we went outside joining our neighbors who had also rushed outside. This made a conversation topic for days to come. Our clocks and pictures were all tipped crooked on the wall. We left them, that was to remind us of the exciting event. The next day while I was in a downtown gift store I asked the lady working there if there had been any damage from the quake? She told me that the only thing disturbed was a gag-gift can that had "Earthquake Can" written on it, it had fallen off a shelf and landed on a display counter below.

Tim returned home to Minnesota during Christmas break in 1995, he left on his fourteenth birthday. The day of the night he was to leave, I came home from school to strange circumstances. When I entered the apartment I noticed several strips of tape on the ceiling near the top of the stairs. Odd, I thought. Further checking I discovered the bathroom floor, upstairs hall carpet, and stair carpet were all wet. Hmm, what could have happened?

Tim was babysitting at Shauns, three doors away. I went over and asked him what had happened. He said he was taking a bath and fell asleep flooding the bathroom. He told me the water was running downstairs onto the couch and floor. He noticed the ceiling was sagging in the corner above the couch, so he put tape on it to keep it from falling! It worked, it didn't fall.

We got everything dried and back in shape, after all, what could I do, it was his fourteenth birthday and that night he was leaving to go home for Christmas vacation?

Tim next to locked moose antlers,
Glennallen, Alaska, August 16, 1995

Tim and Tom NOT looking at the flowers,
Matanuska Glacier, Alaska, August 16, 1995

Wolf on Denali Park Road, August 18, 1995

Chapter 13

That Christmas I was invited out to Jerome's brother and wife's home (former owner of Kantishna Roadhouse) Jerome was also there and I took some pictures of everyone. My motive was to get a picture of Jerome, I thought he was pretty nice and good looking too!

Again it would be necessary to seek work for the next summer. Tom decided he would stay in Fairbanks throughout the upcoming summer. Through inquiring and research I located a lodge that sounded like an interesting place to work, I scheduled a interview with the lodge owner. They would be coming into Fairbanks on business in a few days. After a successful interview I was hired as housekeeper at a very remote lodge at Lake Minchumina, a large lake just outside of the northwest boarder of Denali National Park. Tim and I would be going there in May.

Shaun continued to play practical jokes on me. She used her sense of humor when ever she could to give me a bad time.

She would write notes on large pieces of paper in large print, pretending she was a guy referring to an upcoming date. She would get quite explicit about what clothing, describing some skimpy outfit, that I should wear for this so-called date. She would sign it, "Your Snoogums, Eduardo." This she would tape to the door on the outside of my apartment, for all who were passing by, to see. I know many neighbors and university maintenance people read these notes. She thought it was quite funny, ya it was!! I saved those notes and when I run across them they provide a few good chuckles.

One time while I was at her apartment she called my place and knew the answering machine would come on. There was an maintenance man doing some work in my apartment near the telephone, so he could hear this message without any problem. Shaun called disguised her voice, making it deep, and called about an up-coming date I was to have with this "voice." Well, it was pretty funny. I don't doubt but what that maintenance man didn't stop his hammer in midair when he heard the message.

Tim will always remember an incident that happened while he was in Alaska. I came home from my classes one day, Tim was sitting on the couch, bare feet on the coffee table, with a look of bewilderment on his face. He looked at me. I said, "Tim why aren't you in school?"

He said, "Grandma, I couldn't find my socks."

I thought ya, what is this all about. After searching we discovered there weren't any socks to be found. Tom had taken some of his things, and apparently inadvertently all the socks, when he went to stay with a friend.

Now I wondered how I could send an absent excuse to the junior high school principal, "Absent because he couldn't find his socks"?

Chapter 14

Our friends, Bruce and Bonni who lived in the Alaskan Range Mountains, invited us to visit them during spring break, March 10-16, 1996. Tim and I planned and packed for our upcoming trip to visit our friends in the Bush. Bonni told me to contact Ray Atkins in Cantwell to be flown to the Burnells. I set up the day and time for us to go to the mountains. Ray was one of the few pilots who would fly into this remote location. This area did not have any road access. Burnells usually fly in and out of their place, but have traveled it by snowmobile and dog sled. Once they are in there for the winter they do not usually come out until spring. Bonni worked in the Chalet Gift Shop during the summer and Bruce drove bus in the Park.

March 10, 1996 Tim and I boarded the Alaska Railroad passenger train and headed south toward Cantwell. Along with us we took fresh fruit, meat and fresh vegetables, these items were not easy for Bruce and Bonni to obtain.

Ray met us at the train stop. He lived a short distance

79

from the railroad. While he was making final preparations for our flight, Diane, his wife, invited us in for hot cocoa.

Another new experience for Tim, he had never been in a small plane. The flight was less than an hour. We landed, not on an airstrip, but a clearing in the brush, barely long enough for a plane to land and stop. Both Tim and I were impressed with Ray's ability to land in such a remote place.

Our things were unloaded and stacked in the snow along the clearing. In about half of an hour Bruce and Bonni appeared with their dog sleds to get us. Greetings were exchanged, then Ray flew out. We loaded our cargo and ourselves on the dog sleds. Off we went through the brush and woods bumping along headed to our host's home.

Their log cabin was one room, 12 feet by 16 feet, with a bed in one corner, the table in an adjacent corner, the kitchen area, and a door on opposite end of the cabin The heating barrel stove was to the right when entering the cabin. The cook stove was between the kitchen area and sitting area, with the bed in the corner. The cabin was cozy and comfortable.

The dogs were put back by their houses, fed and given fresh bedding, they were well fed and cared for. They remain there when not out running. The dogs are always anxious to pull the sled and run. Bruce and Bonni had about a dozen dogs, since each of them each have their own dog team.

We quickly were made to feel at home as we unpacked our food items. Bonni showed us to the nearby sauna building where Tim and I would sleep. There was a twin bed as well as a mattress for the floor, a chest of drawers and closet space. A stove and sauna area was to the left of the door. In the sauna part was a shower that had water heated for it through the wood stove.

Our first night it was -25 degrees F. Neither Tim nor I were successful at getting the wood stove to burn, I guess we had both been in the city too long. We were mighty cold by morning.

Bruce and Bonni told us the next morning when we went shivering into the cabin, that we should have went in and asked them for help. We didn't want to bother them, besides once we were covered up we didn't want to climb out to where it was even colder!

Tim got a lesson on starting and keeping a wood stove burning. A big help was sawdust soaked in oil for fire starting. Tim got really good at making a fire; this posed another problem for us, the sauna building did not have any windows. When Tim got a roaring fire going and we were bedded down, we were too hot. We spent the next night with me telling Tim to "open the door a little to cool off the room, then close the door, its getting cold." More wood had to be added to the stove during the night. Tim had been shown how to do the stove so he got to put the wood in. Why should I get up during the night when Tim was the one so eager to be in charge of the stove? I don't believe he always shared that view, however.

After a couple of nights, Tim became less than thrilled at me telling him to open the door because it was too hot, then close it because it was too cold, or that I heard a noise outside. After all, bear or wolves may have gotten us at any time!

Tim finally devised a system that would be easier than getting up each time to open or shut the door. He found a long stick he used to push the door open and pull it back to close the door, at my command, with only a slight grunt. By our last night he had it figured out quite well. During our week there the temperatures remained quit mild, not a repeat of our first night.

Burnell's home was heated with wood, light was provided with oil lamps. The wood cook stove was used for heating water as well as cooking. Both Bruce and Bonni did the cooking, I was impressed with the food that Bonni turned out in such a small working space. She baked bread, cakes, pies, and cookies which appeared to be with little effort. Bonni often uses a head lamp when she cooks. It is a battery operated light with an elastic band on it to fit around the head, holding the light in place on the forehead.

Bruce made delicious pancakes, cooked directly on the stove top. He also cooked steaks over the open flame after removing the round stove top lids. Chest type coolers were used for food storage. Once they were at their cabin, seldom were any other items brought to them. They did have a mail drop three or four times during the winter, which was done by Ray at $300 per mail drop. Without direct communication, there needed to be planning before they went to their cabin in regard to when they would get their mail, as well as to when they would leave their home for their summer employment, this was set up with Ray.

Our stay was filled with new experiences, we enjoyed reading by oil lamp as well as playing board games. The everyday chores, included household duties, caring for the dogs as well as preparing for the next winter. Tim and Bruce worked at hauling, cutting up, and stacking firewood for the next winter.

Every night two or three dogs were brought into the cabin to be played with and given some special attention. Each dog displayed their own distinct personality, some wanted more attention than others. Tim especially enjoyed the dogs, he quickly learned their names and had his favorite, an all white one named Yukon. Me, on the other hand, am not a dog person so I was not as eager to participant in the activities with the dogs.

Each evening at about 9:30 the battery operated radio was turned on for a few minutes. North Pole radio station had a program called "Trapline", this was a special broadcast for individuals without telephones or access to one. Messages and greetings were sent or called into the radio station by the sender. These were read over the air and received by Bush listeners. When I was in Fairbanks I sent special greetings to Bruce and Bonni, letting them know that I was thinking about them.

82

Emergency messages, general information as well as hello messages were sent to an array of people. This is a courtesy service done by Alaskan radio stations.

Without a well or sewer system water was obtained from a spring about a quarter of a mile away and hauled back to the cabin, for the dogs as well as the people. An outhouse was an important building too. Burnells had a cache that was a cabin-like structure up on tall pole legs, which Bruce had built. This prevented predators from getting into it and destroying food or supplies.

The snow cover was less than Bruce and Bonni needed to successfully run their dog team very much. Therefore we did not go on any trips away from the area, short distances like to get water and to the air plane clearing were as far as they went while we were there.

When I made the plans to go to Burnells, I also set up the day and time to be picked up. That day was to be Saturday March 16, 1996. During the night before our departure was a heavy snowfall. The sky was bright blue and clear, pierced by the surrounding Alaskan Range Mountains on that Saturday morning. The previous week had been cloudy, this caused concern as to whether or not Ray would be able to fly in. There was no mistake about the flying conditions on that morning, however. We noticed that morning that there were fresh wolf tracks about 100 feet from the cabin. These tracks trailed off across the new fallen snow into the woods.

With all our things packed we rode in the dog sleds to the clearing to wait for Ray who arrived near the preset time. He came in a smaller plane this time, having concern about taking off in deep snow. His plane was equipped with skis to land in the snow. Ray packed the plane with our belongings and then asked who wanted to be first? Tim and I could not both leave at the same time, because of the snow conditions, weight was a concern. Tim went first, they flew to a remote larger air strip at a lodge some fifteen miles away. Ray soon returned to get me then we met up with Tim.

For both of us to fit into this small plane Tim sat on my lap! The flight back to Cantwell was about half an hour or so. Several times Ray pointed out caribou herds below. We landed smoothly on the air strip back in Cantwell. With our things loaded from the plane to Ray's pickup we waited near the tracks for the train.

The passenger train, between Fairbanks and Anchorage, was on the winter schedule. Southbound Fairbanks to Anchorage on Sundays, north bound from Anchorage to Fairbanks on Saturday. Our plans and scheduling had worked out perfectly.

Tim and I rode the train back to Fairbanks chattering about our exciting experience we had had at a remote mountain cabin; an experience that will be long remembered by both of us.

On the train ride, both ways, the train stopped after it had hit a moose. Around a thousand moose are killed by the train each year along the entire train route. Quite a few are also hit and killed by road traffic. There are signs several places along the highway with an update of the number of moose that have been killed on the highway during a season. People can have their name on a list so when a moose is killed, the state officials notify them and they can go and get the moose for meat. They are required to get the moose, butcher, cut, and process the meat however they want to. The person getting the meat can can the meat, freeze it, or prepare it however they wish. The lists are called by both the railroad and the state for moose.

Bruce gave Tim a large moose antler. He was thrilled over this gift. A moose antler is not the easiest to pack and carry, so the best way to pack it was not to. He just carried it along with our other things, fitting it in spaces and crannies in Ray's airplane. There wasn't a problem with this antler (half of a set) until it came time for Tim to go back to Minnesota. How was he to pack such an awkward thing to board the airplane? It was evident it would not fit in a suitcase or even a box he was taking with him. He certainly couldn't carry it "as is" on the airplane. He had carried it on the train and got a lot of stares and comments. He didn't want it to go as a piece of luggage, using one of his luggage allotments. So he left it with me, with the promise I would mail it.

The day came when I got serious about mailing the antler. I couldn't find a box it would fit into without the box being very large. So I fit a box around the antler. Folding, bending, and crushing down the box to form around the odd form, took not only hand work, but foot work, along with a good deal of Duct Tape. I managed to master the task.

I wondered what the postal clerks were thinking when they saw the odd sculpture-like package? There was a strong temptation to print in large letters "GLASS", on this grotesque configuration. I wish I would have, the post office clerks' reaction would have been worth it.

Bonni and Bruce by their cabin, March 16, 1996

Bonni cooking with headlamp, March 11, 1996

Steaks cooking on wood stove, March 12, 1996

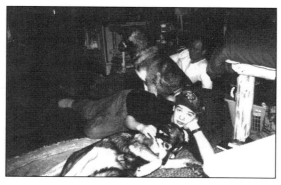

Bruce and Tim with sled dogs, March 14, 1996

Author in dogsled, March 16, 1996

DeVonne, Tim and Ray leaving Alaska Range,
March 16, 1996

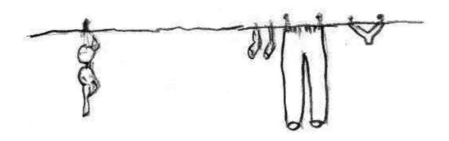

Chapter 15

My journal refers to May 15, 1996 as a red letter day. It was the day Tom took Tim and I to the airport to get a plane to go to Lake Minchumina, Alaska. This plane was a small passenger plane, holding less than six people. We were at the airport at 7:30 A.M. for a 8:00 A.M. departure. We arrived at Lake Minchumina some time a little after 9:00 A.M., which is 139 air miles from Fairbanks.

Tim and I got off the plane at the Lake Minchumina airstrip, (no airport). We had no idea what direction or how/where to go. There were four other people there. They asked me where we were going. I said, "Darned if I know!"

I did tell them we were headed for the lodge, but didn't know which direction or how far it was. We were told it was about six miles or so that way as they pointed in an easterly direction.

I had not packed a lunch or brought any water. A man who had been on the plane with us gave us his bottle of water.

A lady there told us she would walk with us for a mile or so. I thought, ya, then what? We walked with her until her driveway. About that time Bruce from the lodge met us. We walked about three and a half miles with Bruce to a canoe. We rode in the canoe for a ways, we then went ashore and walked further meeting up with Jason, who was also from the lodge. Jason was waiting in a boat for us.

Several times during our boat ride the two guys had to climb out of the boat onto the ice and push the boat over the ice back into open water. Tim and I sat in the boat through this procedure. When we got to the lodge at the dock we climbed into a trailer being pulled by a four-wheeler for a ride about a half a mile up the hill to the lodge.

Tim and I were exhausted when we got there. The owners were not there, they were due back the next day. One of the workers made us feel welcome, she was suggesting things for us to do--we didn't want to do anything. She suggested we could go for a walk, there was a lot to see and that it was really pretty there. I looked at her and said, "What makes you think I could possibly want to go for a walk?" As my journal states "My, my, what a day." All the procedures we had gone through to get there made me wonder if civilization had been left in a different world, would we even see another soul while at what seemed like "the last place on earth?"

We soon fell into a routine, I started getting the lodge building, laundry house, sauna, and cabins ready for summer guests. Tim helped out with yard work, he planted grass, cleaned the yard and hauled garbage and generally helped out.

One day he burned two of his fingers quite bad on the muffler of the four-wheeler. If we had been closer to town he would have been taken to the doctor. But the lodge owner cleaned it and cared for it each day, checking to make sure it didn't become infected. If any problem had arisen Tim would have been flown to Fairbanks for medical treatment. His fingers healed nicely without any problems.

Our belongings were stored in a building at the airstrip, the day we went to the lodge it was not possible to take them with us as we walked. On May 21, when one of the guys went across the lake, about six miles in a boat, to get the mail, he brought our things to us.

I was the only housekeeper. On my one day off a week, if there was a cabin to be cleaned one of the other workers did it. Laundry, sauna cleaning, as well as all my other work was done on my working days. I did all the owners personal laundry as well. They had a small girl who delighted in changing her clothes many times a day as well as drag around towels, all which had to be washed after she threw them down, wherever! That often kept me busy, as she was allowed to do as she pleased, even if it meant added work for someone.

There were seven outhouses to clean, along with four cabins, one a very large cabin. There was not any electricity to the cabins, so I had to string long extension cords from the electric source in order to plug in the vacuum cleaner. Two cabins had stone floors. The vacuum cleaner was quite heavy and these floors were difficult to vacuum. The cabins with stone floors, often had mushrooms or grass sprout up between the rocks on the floor. These two cabins also had sod roofs, Tim planted flowers on them, he thought it was pretty neat to plant flowers upon a sod roof.

The outhouses had to be kept free of cobwebs, dust and dirt. Each needed to always be stocked with an adequate supply of toilet tissue, reading material, as well as a coffee can full of ashes, from the sauna stove, to be put down the hole to cut down on odor.

Nearly all summer it was possible to hang all the laundry outside to dry, I seldom needed to use the clothes dryer. I noted in my journal that July 13, was the first time I had to dry the laundry in the clothes dryer. With all the other work it was an added task to carry the laundry out and gather it in again. On occasion it was necessary to quickly get the laundry in when it started to rain.

The sauna had a shower on each end with a wood stove in between. On the roof were two water tanks one was a barrel the other an old chest-type freezer. Water to fill the tanks came from a hose that was strung across the yard and then carried up onto the roof, by way of a ladder, put into the containers on the roof and filled. The well was down by the lake, water was pumped up into a water tank which was up high in the air behind the lodge building, that was where all the water was for use at the lodge.

It was necessary for me to keep a fire going in the sauna stove so there would be hot water for guest showers or saunas. The sauna building needed regular cleaning and kept stocked with towels. I was the only one who did the work in the sauna building.

There were a lot of flowers, planters, and flower beds. I kept those watered and free of dead flowers and leaves. There was a large garden with a variety of fresh vegetables that was used for guest meals. Tim and I also did some garden work. Another duty I had was assisting with breakfast in the mornings. The guests were provided with meals in the family-style dining area of the lodge. Ten guests were usually the most there at one time, staying five to seven days. I also assisted with the evening meal when needed.

A generator provided the lodge with electricity as well as the employee's cabins, each night the generator was turned off to conserve fuel. Cooking was done on a gas stove as well as a wood cook stove.

Early in the season the sled dogs were taken from the lodge to two families across the lake, for the summer. The dogs were loaded in a boat, this required several trips across the lake. It was quite a sight to see a boat (row boat type) loaded with several dogs and people going across the lake disappearing in the distance while listening to the dogs protest loudly and attempting to get out of the boat.

At the end of May Tim and some of the workers from the lodge began taking a first aid and CPR class. They went across the lake each day to attend the class. In such an isolated area it is best if nearly everyone knows basic first aid and CPR. Tim completed his first aid and CPR class and earned his card.

In June there was a black bear at the lodge, I got pictures of it as I observed it in the trees near my cabin. The bear made several visits, some guests as well as the workers enjoyed watching this fellow. One Sunday afternoon I was at the lodge alone, everyone else had gone across the lake to a community ball game. I heard the dog making a fuss, so I checked it out. I could see the bear in the woods in front of my cabin. I wanted to get pictures of it, so I went around behind all the cabins and into mine, where I could observe the bear quite well.

During the summer supplies were flown in and then brought across by boat. In the wintertime snowmobiles were used for transportation. In this tiny community of about thirty people there were only a couple of trucks, and I didn't see any cars. There was not any place of distance to drive to. Four-wheelers were the main way to get around in the summer. There was a post office that received mail several times a week. Lake Minchumina had a school and a store, which were not open while I was there.

Guests came from foreign countries including Canada and also from the lower forty eight states and Hawaii. The guests enjoyed excellent food in an unique Alaskan setting. They were taken fishing, flight seeing, hiking, boat riding, camping, on a visit to a Native village, as well as having a presentation by some of the local people about living in the Bush.

Tim's stay in Alaska would soon be ending. His mother had agreed he could stay until school was out in May. We successfully talked her into letting him stay until sometime in June. After all he did not want to miss the opportunity to go to a remote lodge for a couple months. After Tim talked with his mom, a date was decided on, and his mom said he could stay until the end of June. She missed him and wanted him back home. He told me, "Grandma, I would have picked June 31, to go home, but there isn't one, so I'll go home June 30." It wasn't that he did not want to go home, he just didn't want to leave Alaska!

Tim left before the end of June to spend some time with his Uncle Tom in Fairbanks. At the lodge we all reluctantly saw him off, he had been an added joy to the lodge. He helped out with chores and enjoyed the company of the owner's son.

I often commented that Tim's mom would have had a "fit" if she had known ahead of time about all the adventures Tim had. When she heard after the fact there was not much she could say. But I am sure she often wondered, "What is Mom doing with my son?!" Of course Tim loved every minute of his stay in Alaska and all the adventures he experienced. He said he plans on coming back when he graduates from high school.

In July Tom came to spend a few days with me. One afternoon we took a canoe and went fishing. We caught thirteen northern pike. We decided that was an unlucky number so we caught another one. As we caught them we threw them back, keeping two to eat later. When we got back to the lodge it was near midnight, but still very much daylight out. The lodge was empty, everyone was asleep in cabins. Tom cleaned and fried the fish so we had a scrumptious late night snack.

My summer at Lake Minchumina ended in late July. I returned to Fairbanks to the cabin Tom and I had rented about nine miles north of town. It was an unfurnished cabin without water. We hauled water from the spring north of Fox, which is north of Fairbanks. It did have electricity, telephone, bottled gas for the cook stove and an oil heater.

Dogs being taken across lake Minchumina,
May 29, 1996

Water tanks on sauna building, June 23, 1996

Chapter 16

On July 27, I was home alone after getting comfortable in my pajamas and was watching TV. About 11:00 P.M. I went to the outhouse, and upon returning I discovered I had locked myself out. The windows were high from the ground, the cabin being upon posts with steps leading to the one door. The steps, however, were not wide enough to extend below the window.

What was I to do? There wasn't anyone nearby, besides where would I go in my pajamas? I found an old chair behind the cabin as well as an orange highway marker cone. Putting the cone on the chair I then managed to climb on top of the teetering stack. I hoisted myself up to the small open window. The screen was loose and easy to push aside. Inside, a chest of drawers sat just under the window.

Easy! All I had to do was crawl through the window. Sometimes things in life are not as easy as they first appear--this was one of those times. With my upper half inside the cabin and the rest of me remaining outside, I tried to pull my leg up into the window. I could not get it in! After a few attempts I pondered my situation. Many ideas ran through my mind, none of which were useful to me after careful consideration.

After several minutes, (these awkward situations always last, in ones mind, for hours,) my attention was drawn to the TV, which was directly across from the window, by a special announcement. No, it was not about a woman stuck in a window in Alaska. The announcement was about the Atlantic City bombing. This held my attention for a period of time, with my elbows on the dresser top, head in hands, bottom half outside, I stopped my struggles to watch the television.

I knew I needed to get, **all of me**, back into the cabin before the bombing case was solved and before Tom got home. I would have never lived it down if Tom had came home to find his mother hanging out/in the cabin window at midnight. No amount of explaining would have been listened to. Besides he may have friends with him.

With these scary thoughts I once again began my struggle. I managed to attempt all the maneuvers of an experienced contortionist without success. I finally twisted myself and somehow got though the window, **all of me**. Climbing down off the dresser I was elated at my accomplishment. I have no idea which move was the right one and certainly did not want to repeat that episode again.

When Tom came home I related my experience to him. He said he had done the same thing, only he hoisted himself up to the kitchen window and climbed into the sink. The kitchen window was a larger one but much higher from the ground. I had looked at that as a possibility, but could not reach it even on my cobbled up climbing apparatus.

Chapter 17

Once again school time was fast approaching. We decided to find an apartment in Fairbanks. August 1, 1996 we moved into a nice two bedroom apartment. We quickly settled in and had a month to enjoy a little free time before school started. Tom was working with a man who installed rain gutters on houses. He wouldn't be doing this during the winter and they would soon finish up their work.

Tom and I had been invited to visit the Koppenberg Gold Mine located at about 74 miles on the Steese Highway, north east of Fairbanks, then three miles to Faith Creek where the mine was located.

We left early Saturday morning which was September 7, 1996. The trees were wearing their bright fall colors they graced the roadside with all their beauty. We had a most enjoyable trip up through this beautiful area.

Bruce and Bonni also visited the mine, they arrived shortly after we did. We waited for them at Faith Creek and rode across the creek with them. We had a borrowed car and did not want to drive it into the creek. Tom's friend had borrowed Tom's truck so we had his friend's car.

We were met and greeted by the Koppenbergs at the mine. We were shown to a bus that was remodeled into a very nice camper. It had a double bed in the back end, bunk bed sets on each side by the windows, to provide sleeping space for four. Next was a stove, the counter top, sink and refrigerator on one side. On the other side after the bunk beds the counter tops lead to the door with a oil heating stove next to the door. Bruce and Bonni slept in the back bed area, Tom and I had the bunk beds, where we were quite comfortable.

The next day we went out to see the mining operation which was an impressive set up. Dale Koppenberg operated the huge equipment that dug the dirt, placing it into the big plant, (trommel) which turned and sifted out the rocks on a long conveyor belt. The gold drops through the screen into something called the sluice box. The larger rocks drop off the end of the screen onto the conveyor which deposits them onto a large pile. Water washed over the dirt and rocks as part of the separation process. Jerome Koppenberg did the work on the ground, moving water pipes, moving the plant, and an array of other duties. Dale spent all his time in the big backhoe.

Several moves were made during the 10 hour, seven day a week mining process. After the gold fell onto what is referred to as "the carpets," it is taken up to the main camp for screening. This is a process in which several round pan-type containers with screen in the bottom are used to further separate the gold from the dirt. This is done using several sizes of pans working up to a very fine-screened pan.

The next step was called boxing, a long trough made of metal with a grate in the bottom was place in an incline position from the back of the van (a truck van), to the ground. Water at a precise flow ran into this trough and the screened gold was placed, using a kitchen serving spoon, into the trough. The water then separated the gold from most of the remaining dirt and deposited it at the end. Dirt being lighter than gold, would wash onto the ground.

Then the gold was taken and put on a large gold wheel which is grooved and slanted to separated the gold from the final particles of dirt. This process is done with water also.

The final stage was drying the gold, in gold pans, on the gas cook stove in the house, then they weighed the gold. This is done on very accurate balance-type scales, scales used for precious metals. When this is completed the gold is taken to the smelter. All this process is called the cleanup and is done every fifty hours or about every five days. This was always an exciting time, they were able to see how much gold had been mined at the end of each fifty hours of work.

Jerome usually did the screening and boxing, sometime the wheel process too. Dale did the drying and weighing of the gold. The mining season was from mid-June to the end of September.

Tom and I were totally amazed at all the gold we saw. We could hardly believe our eyes. This was truly an exceptional experience, one we would always remember.

We returned to Fairbanks with tales of our experience for friends who were anxious to hear about our big weekend at a real gold mine.

Chapter 18

School started once again for us. Tom was a freshman at the university and I was a second year senior. I had done elementary school student teaching then changed my major to Early Childhood Development. Tom took freshman requirement classes as well as art classes.

For Christmas that year I went back to visit family and friends in Minnesota. Before I left I sent a picture I had taken of Jerome the previous year, in a Christmas card to Cantwell, Alaska, where he lived. I included my phone number and suggested he call me sometime when he came to Fairbanks.

When I went back to Minnesota I took one of the pictures of Jerome to show people I visited, hinting of my interest in Jerome. I was in Minnesota nearly a month. The roads were icy and driving conditions were poor. Interstate 94 was closed completely across the state. I could not visit all the people I wanted to. At times I could not even leave St. Cloud, where I was staying with my daughter Cheryl and her family. I said I wanted to go home where the weather was nicer, Fairbanks. Where there was no wind and a person could get around. Two times I had to cancel a rental car because I could not get out of town. However, this did provide me with more time to spend with my oldest daughter, Cheryl and her children, Annie, Tim, Collin, and Alex.

I returned to Fairbanks early in January to start school. This was my last semester, I would be graduating May 11, Mothers Day. Toward the end of January Jerome call me from his home in Cantwell. After talking a while he asked me if I would like to go out? My heart leaped, I was so excited, I had a hope hidden far away that he would call.

Our first night out Jerome took me to the Castle Restaurant in Fairbanks for a lovely dinner. In a week or so he called me again. Jerome lived 170 miles from Fairbanks so frequent trips were difficult, but we did continue to date. Phone calls were made often and were most welcome.

Jerome came to Alaska, in 1950. We were both born in Minnesota, Jerome in Pine River, and I in Bemidji. These two towns are about 60 miles apart. As a child I lived near Shevlin, 25 miles north west of Bemidji. Jerome lived in the Cambridge, Prinston, Minnesota area as well as Pine River. We did not know each other until we met in Alaska, nearly 4,000 miles away and many years later.

One of the first jobs he had in Alaska was working on building a bridge near Palmer, Alaska. That bridge has recently been replaced with a new one.

April 24, I was honored to attend a ceremony for Golden Key Honor Society, of which I am a member. I was pleased with my accomplishment of maintaining a straight 'A' average in order to become a member.

I was busy with school, but Tom wanted me to go mud bogging with him in his pickup, so I promised him I would go May 4th. It was an activity all his friends liked to do. Somewhere south of Fairbanks in the river bottom area is where this activity took place. I took my cameras along and enjoyed the ride. Of course one of the main events was getting stuck in the mud and pulling each other out, which was done quite a few times. They would see how far they could get without getting stuck. Tom's friends, Joe Muegel and Amanda Thomas were there in their car, as well as Jason McGahey, another friend in his pickup. I got some good videos and we had a good time. When we left, the pickup was encased in mud. This brought looks and points from other drivers when we got back to Fairbanks.

Chapter 19

Jerome expressed an interest in attending my graduation, which was coming up soon. Final preparations were made for my graduation and the big day arrived. We had practiced the procedure the day before. The day of graduation we were all in our places as a class. The university gymnasium was full as were the bleachers, with families and friends of those graduating.

When I was called to receive my diploma I proceeded up the aisle onto the stage, received my diploma and walked to the other side and down the steps. When I reached the bottom I drew a complete blank in front of hundreds of people, where was I supposed to go? I turned to Helena Scherder who was behind me, I asked her which direction were we supposed to go? She shrugged her shoulders and didn't know either!

Now I believe the chances of two people, who had not paid attention to directions given the day before, being together are slim, but it had happened to us. With Helena following me

I knew I needed to go some place, so I started down the aisle directly in front of me. When I got near the back of the gymnasium there was only two places to go, out the door or squeeze between two rows of attentive guests. I chose the latter. Excusing ourselves we side-stepped our way past these people, not unlike leaving the middle of a row in a movie theater. By this time we were nearly overcome with laughter (silent). We quickly got across the row and sat down with a big sigh of relief. I was tapped on the shoulder by a classmate behind me asking, "What are you doing there?" We were in the wrong row!!!

Instead of the aisle I had chosen, we were supposed to have walked back below and in front of the stage and returned down the aisle we had came up. From the bleachers Tom and Jerome were watching our fiasco. Tom had video taped me until I got part way down the wrong aisle. I believed he stopped to watch in wonderment--where was mom going? Jerome later said he thought I was leaving!

Chapter 20

The day after graduation Jerome took me to his place, 25 miles south of Cantwell. It was a beautiful drive, this early spring time in Alaska. He lived two miles off the Parks Highway on the shore of Colorado Lake. Colorado Lake being on one side of the house and a large pond on the other. The beautiful Talkeetna Mountains reflected in the pond in front of the house. The Alaska Mountain Range was in the distance across Colorado Lake with a tip of Mt. McKinley visible from the steps of the house. Truly a gorgeous place on this narrow strip of land between the lake and pond.

While standing in the yard near the house, one could throw a stone either into the lake or pond. Beyond the house the area wet lands blend into the pond and lake. There was not a road directly to Jerome's home. We drove in to the railroad crossing, which is across the lake, entering through a private locked crossing. We then drove along the lake until coming to the railroad siding. Here we left the pickup, walked across the rail tracks, then Jerome drove us on his four-wheeler around the end of the lake along the far side of the pond and back between pond and lake to his house. This trip was about one and a half miles. On our way around the lake we saw a pair of beautiful swans swimming in the water, they were truly magnificent birds.

This quiet setting provided a tranquil peaceful place to live. It took extra effort to get there but it was worth it. Jerome had moved his things this way, making many trips with the four-wheeler and trailer.

I enjoyed my visit at Jerome's home. During that time he asked me to marry him. I accepted and we set our wedding date for Friday June 13, 1997. Jerome's birthday is April 1, so we thought Friday the 13th would be fitting for our wedding date. Plans were made for our wedding to be at the Koppenberg Gold Mine at Faith Creek.

We visited Jerome's mom, Lola Koppenberg in Big Lake, Alaska to tell her about our upcoming wedding, she was happy for us. At that time I also met his sister Thelma Koppenberg, niece Laurie Rowe husband Jim, and son Lyle.

Tom was thrilled to learn of our upcoming marriage. He too had visited Jerome at Colorado Lake. He and Jerome spent time together and enjoyed each others company. Tom helped with clean-up in the dock area of the lake as well as some yard cleaning.

Chapter 21

The day of our wedding we got last minute items in Fairbanks including our wedding cake. We had previously ordered it with specific instructions that it needed to be assembled to withstand a 77 mile trip of which 37 miles would be gravel road.

We picked up the cake and headed out of town. All was well for most of the travel on the tarred portion of the road. Disaster then began to set in. I was keeping an eye on the cake setting in the extended cab section of the pickup. I started to notice small shifts in the three tier cake, I attempted to shift it to keep it from tipping and sliding.

It was evident that the cake was going to be a challenge for us. I told Jerome we needed to stop and see if we could stabilize the cake. With that he turned into the next driveway. The abrupt turn accelerated the cakes' sliding process. I grabbed the top as it continued to disengage itself from the bottom. When we stopped, I was half twisted in the seat with my fingers embedded in the frosting. (Remember we had picked

Friday the thirteenth for our wedding!) Jerome and I tried to figure out how we could stabilize the cake. Finally Jerome decided to go and cut some willow sticks to attempt to insert them into the cake layers. But, the sticks would not go beyond the first layer.

In desperation I wanted to hold onto the cake the best I could and keep shifting it into place. By this time we had well sampled the frosting. The frosting had gotten many places besides on the cake! We arrived at the mine looking like we had been in a food fight. Frosting was on the pickup seats, steering wheel, interior walls, our clothes as well as our faces and hands. The cake was quickly taken into the house and went through a reconstruction process. Pictures taken later did not reveal a hint of its condition a short time earlier.

When it came time for us to cut the cake, we could not bring ourselves to smear each other with cake and frosting as new brides and grooms sometimes do, we had experienced that earlier.

Upon examining the construction of the cake we discovered the layers were placed on slippery pieces of cardboard. Nothing was holding the layer in place, therefore they slid apart.

The day before our wedding we left a copy of the vows we had written for our wedding ceremony with Jerome's brother, other family members and friends. The ceremony was scheduled for 3:00 P.M., giving family and friends time to get to the mine from Fairbanks.

The big moment arrived for me to leave the house, with Tom at my side, we walked out to join Jerome, the wedding party, and guests. As we walked out the *Wedding March* was being played, then suddenly it changed to *The Old Gray Mare*. I soon realized what had happened to the written ceremony words I had entrusted the family and friends with the previous day. They had rewritten the ceremony!

In Alaska any adult can be commissioned to perform a

marriage ceremony. To have a friend or relative do it makes it more special. Jerome's brother preformed our ceremony, was in charge of the video camera and played music on his accordion. A shotgun was shot and a small cannon fired. Our shotgun wedding brought laughter and joy to everyone.

True, marriage is serious, be we felt it wasn't necessary for it to start with a solemn, glum, long drawn-out ceremony that most everyone dislikes sitting through. Of course this is a personal choice. We chose to be married by a relative with a few close friends and relatives. Due to the distance, most of our relatives and friends were not able to attend. Tom was my only relative there.

We received many nice cards and gifts. When we were opening gifts we opened one that had a wooden loon in it. This loon, an ornament, had been sitting on top of the cupboard in Jerome's kitchen. Some of his friends decided to play a joke on us and take the loon from the house, wrap it up and give it as a gift. Of course we thought it was funny. But none of them knew just how funny it was. Jerome had received that loon from a previous lady he was dating! I knew about the loon. We kept the loon sitting on the counter in the camper bus for the summer. When it came time to pack up and go home, I accidentally dropped it and broke its head off. I felt bad, because it was an accident, but may have not looked like it. When we got home I talked Jerome into gluing the head back on, he did, but to be funny he put it back on backwards!! None of this about the loon was revealed until I told Chris and Jay one day when they visited us in the fall of 1999.

Joe and Amanda, Tom's close friends, attending our wedding. They were impressed and excited about the uniqueness of our wedding. Joe thought it was great. They later asked Tom to perform their wedding ceremony.

After our wedding we spent the weekend in Fairbanks. We then returned to the mine, moving into the bus. The same bus, remodeled into living quarters, that Tom and I had stayed in the previous September. At that time I had no idea I would be living there as Jerome's wife!

We enjoyed our summer at the mine and spent our spare time reading, playing Yahtzee, and four-wheel rides after Jerome's work day. He showed me the beautiful country, we either went on the four-wheeler or took the pickup.

We spent much time reading. Jerome especially liked reading the hilarious stories from Patrick McManus books. We had many a good laugh from these books.

Late in the summer we saw a black bear around our place. We were at the main house when we observed the bear walking around the camper, peering into the back of the pickup, then back to the camper looking into the windows. The bear looked around then walked off down the road.

Mining went well, Jerome was thrilled to find a two-and-one half ounce gold nugget. It was in with the other finer pieces of gold. Later he found a slightly smaller one.

It is true there is a pot of gold at the end of the rainbow. After a rain shower I took a picture of a rainbow that had one end at the top of the mining plant. This was an unusual sight.

It was unusual to see where the river had been moved in order to mine the ground. The trees and brush were cleared as well. It was an odd sight to see the dry riverbed with the river moved several hundred feet away.

Tom was able to visit us several times during the summer and we always had a good time. He especially liked to watch the mining process. Shaun, from Fairbanks, also visited us.

Bride and groom, Jay Holmberg, Sid Blatchford (holding shotgun),
Amanda Thomas and Joe Muegel in background, June 13, 1997

Gold-mining equipment, July 18, 1997

Jerome at small clean-up box,
August 15, 1997

Gold-mining equipment, July 18, 1997

Jerome holding gold pan, August 14, 1997

Jerome weighing gold, August 15, 1997

Jerome at end of gold clean up, August 15, 1997

Dale and Tom with gold nuggets, September 6, 1997

PART TWO

Chapter 22

At the end of the mining season, which was October 1, we closed up camp and went to Fairbanks. We spent a day there, then hauled some of my belongings to our home at Colorado Lake. We made a couple trips back to Fairbanks to bring my things to my new home. Jerome still had some things stored in Fairbanks. It took us about a year to get all of our things to our home. Each trip to Fairbanks we would bring more back home with us.

During the summer of 1997 a old previous road that had grown over with trees and brush was reopened. When we went back to our home the new road provided a much easier access to our place.

The road certainly makes it much easier to get to and from our home. The trade-off for that is, it is no longer as secluded as it was. There is also the task of keeping the road cleared of snow during the winter. Jerome often does this plowing, At times it took a good portion of a day to get this two mile road cleared.

Life in my new home was exciting as well as challenging. I was now 170 miles from shopping and 25 miles from our mail box! This required major adjustments, but I loved it.

We continued to do a great deal of reading, I especially enjoy Alaskan books. Jerome had many books about Alaska. I continued to learn all I could about this most beautiful, fascinating state, I now call my home.

This was Jerome's second winter at Colorado Lake so he had become used to living in this remote area. It had been more difficult to get supplies and equipment in before the road was opened up. He accomplished it he said, "By brute force and awkwardness." I don't believe the awkwardness part, but certainly the brute force.

The year before I arrived Jerome had done some remodeling. He built a new wooden stairway going upstairs, to replace the steep, narrow metal spiral stairs that were in the center of the living room, leading upstairs. He also installed a toilet stool, moved the bath tub as well as installing a stacking washer and dryer. These things were hauled in from across the railroad tracks by his four-wheeler, in a trailer.

I heard a funny story from some of Jerome's friends. One night Jerome got up to answer nature's call. He decided not to go down stairs and out to the outhouse (before he had the toilet stool installed), so he went out onto the deck that was off from the bedroom to answer the call. Well, when he attempted to return back into the house, the door had swung shut and locked. Here he was outside in the winter with nothing on and the door was locked! There was an escape rope hanging from the deck. He shimmied down that into the snow and around the house into the downstairs door. His friends will never let him forget that event, as if he could!

Jerome built a beautiful bathroom sink cabinet with doors and drawers for the bathroom. Later he made a mirrored cabinet for above the sink. Both are very nice.

There were some problems with the generator. It had stopped running. This caused concern because our heating system was a heater that required electricity. Jerome decided it was necessary to purchase a stove that did not require electricity. In Fairbanks we bought a beautiful oil stove. It was black with a glass door, and three mirrors inside to reflect the burning flame. It is a nice looking addition in our home. It was quite expensive, about $1,500, but well worth it when heat is an important factor. For the months of November through February, 97-98, Jerome averaged the temperature and it had been just slightly below 0 degrees F. That included some twenty or so below 0 degree F weather, with most of the time being above 0 degrees F. It averaged out to be a mild winter. The new oil stove burned about two gallons of fuel a day during that winter.

The stove has a lift-lid to reveal a cook top. We keep this open however. I do nearly all my cooking on this oil stove cook-top. I regulate the cooking temperature by moving the pans to different areas of the stove. Very little cooking is done on the gas range when the heating stove is burning. We have a 2,000 gallon fuel tank. We burn about 3,500 gallons of fuel oil a year, coming to a little over $3,000.

Jerome's sister, Thelma, gave us an electric roaster in which I do all my baking and oven-required cooking. She also, for a wedding gift, gave us a lovely sofa-type love seat.

At Christmas time Jerome went into the woods on his snowmobile and got us a small Christmas tree. It was our first Christmas together, we were snowed in so it was not possible for us to have any company or to go anywhere, so we enjoyed Christmas, just the two of us.

In early January 1998, I observed a weasel romping on the deck. I got my camera and snapped two pictures of the weasel, one going into a hanging wire basket, one when it was coming out. It was fun to watch his quick actions in search of food.

After enduring problems with the generator Jerome decided to purchase a new 20KW (20,000 watt) generator. This came with a price tag of $10,000. He installed it himself. With a larger generator it allows him to run his woodworking tools, saws, routers, planers, etc., and all our electric lights and appliances without stress, as there was on the smaller generator. Electricity isn't required to heat the house except for the heat tape on the well pipe. When it is extremely cold -30 degrees F or colder, there is a danger of pipes freezing. So far we have seldom had such cold temperatures.

A unique feature of having a generator is the use of electricity. We call it free electricity, well sort of. When the generator is running, which is all the time in the winter, all the lights are left turned on. Only our bedroom light is turned off when we go to bed. The generator needs something to do, so it is necessary to keep lights on and use electric appliances frequently. Jerome changes the oil in the generator every ten days and the oil filter every twenty days. When he does this he turns off the generator then all electricity is off, drains out the old oil and replaced it with new oil. In the winter time he will often do this early in the evening when it is dark then we have a candle light supper which is fun for a change of atmosphere.

Whenever we are coming back home in the winter time and are coming down a hill less than one half a mile from home, we say, "Look at all the lights, must be somebody home." Of course there is no one there, but the house is lit up. In the summer time when it is constant daylight the lights are on as well, then we hardly notice them.

The generator also charges a battery pack which runs our 12 volt refrigerator. In the summer time when the generator, often during the night, is off, the battery pack (when fully charged) will keep the refrigerator working. We really like the refrigerator, it does not have a fan in it. That is what seems to cause foods to dry out faster in other types of refrigerators. Inside the refrigerator is solid without vents or openings. There is a small freezer unit in the top, which has separate door. Fresh vegetables will keep for several months. It is also a very quiet running unit.

For heating water we have an on-demand propane heater. There is a thirty gallon water storage tank upstairs which is kept pumped full of cold water by the water from the well. From this we get our household water.

One day in January 1998, while we were in Time-To-Eat, a small cafe in Cantwell, Diana Atkins told us about the seniors meal each Thursday at noon. This sounded like it would be interesting. So our winter social activity, meeting new people and making new friends at the seniors' luncheon became a regular activity for us. Among these people was Ray Atkins who had flown Tim and I to visit the Burnells in the Alaska Range Mountains two years ago.

Winter has its special beauty, the sparkling pure white snow is dazzling in the sun. There is a short time in the fall when we have two sun rises. The sun rises just above the Talkeetna Mountains, but not high enough to be completely above all of them. The sun remains low, then is again behind mountains before appearing.

Winter is a quiet, peaceful, cozy time. I enjoy the shorter days when winter wraps us in snow and colder temperatures. It is a cozy time to be inside beside the fire. It is invigorating to be outside to ski or walk, then come in and enjoy the warmth of our home.

Winter is a time to unwind after the summer flurry of activity. We are often home two weeks or more at a time without seeing anyone or going anyplace. We do not get TV reception, but our VCR provides entertainment by watching videos. We have over a hundred videos and enjoy watching them over several times.

Jay and Chris Holmberg, who live in Palmer, Alaska, visit us when they are up here at their cabin, this is usually on weekends. We do not have any nearby year around neighbors.

117

Cabins across the lake are used for weekends or vacation cabins.

I brought two Alaskan books with me from Minnesota. One of them was *Dog Sled*, by Slim Randall from Talkeetna, Alaska. I hadn't read the book before I brought it. While reading the book I was under the impression it was a true account, as it had stated it was. But as I read along I came to a chapter that told about the writer coming to the home of George Goble in Cantwell, Alaska. Now I thought this was ridiculous, I thought this was suppose to be true and everyone knows the comedian George Goble does not live in Cantwell, Alaska.

I continued reading and finished the book with a different view of the story. Several days after finishing the book we met a man who was staying at a cabin across the lake. He said his name was Radar (Raymond) and in conversation he mentioned his dad. I asked him what was his dad's name? Radar said, "George Goble." I realized I had been wrong about the book there was a George Goble in Cantwell!

We became acquainted with George and his wife Pat, they too attended the senior luncheons in Cantwell I asked Pat about the book *Dog Sled*. She didn't know about it, they didn't know George was in the book. They remembered the visit from the author in about 1969. George and Pat read the book and were surprised to find the part about George in it.

It is a delightful, funny book. The author endures trials and hardships while attempting to run a dog sled. He makes the accounts hilarious. It is one of my favorite Alaskan books.

During our first winter at Colorado Lake we began listening to the radio, getting only one station, KTNA, public broadcasting station. Saturday night we enjoyed *Prairie Home Companion*, with Garrison Keeler, Sunday night Girls Night Out, with Denise Scott and her daughter Chari. We were impressed with their program and what a good job twelve-year old Chari did on the radio. Their program was a music program taking requests, Jerome and I often called and requested songs for each other. They also had a "guess who" segment in their program. We both enjoyed that, I often correctly guessed the music artist, which entitled me to win a candy bar Denise and Chari would give away to the winner. Twice we stopped in at the radio station to get the candy bar, on our way to Big Lake. Most of the time they sent me the candy in the mail. I believe I won about eleven times, I decided to just listen most of the time and let others have a chance.

When we come home from Fairbanks or Cantwell we enjoy stopping at the Igloo. It was a service station with candy, pop, and souvenirs. It is about three miles from our home. We liked to talk to people who stopped there, some travelers, others were people who had weekend cabins across the lake from us. The Igloo has snacks and beverages for sale. It no longer sells gas or souvenirs, it may sometime in the future. Along the Parks Highway there is a distance of 95 miles where gas cannot be purchased.

We live in an area of about 15,200 square miles here there are only about twenty people living! This area is from mile 134 on the Parks Highway north to mile 209, and about 100 miles on each side of the highway. Along this stretch there are three businesses, two at which a meal can be purchased, all have rooms to rent for the traveler, in the winter time these are closed.

We are located nearly half way between Fairbanks and Anchorage. We prefer to do all our shopping, medical care, and business in Fairbanks. A few times during the year we go to Big Lake, Palmer, and Wasilla to visit family and friends. We also do some shopping then too.

My son Tom resides in Fairbanks, he is a certified welder at Greer Tank. I try to spend a few days visiting him each fall. Because of the distance it is difficult for him to visit us. Whenever we travel to Fairbanks it always includes a visit with Tom.

119

Author with grosbeak, October 23, 1997

Grosbeak on outside thermometer, January 12, 1998

Jerome by new generator, January 27, 1998

Chapter 23

Winter is my favorite time of the year. It is so incredibly peaceful and serene out in the beautiful wilderness, I enjoy all this by skiing daily. Al Batten, a man in Fairbanks who worked at the museum where I volunteered at the herbarium, gave me a pair of skis and ski boots. One night after Jerome and I had gone to bed I could see the moonlight through the bedroom door window. I decided to get up and go for a moonlight ski, it was great, I skied around the pond, taking about half an hour. I wanted to repeat this, but whenever there was a full moon it was cloudy so that kept me from skiing at night, I hope to do it again.

Jerome got me a pair of electric, battery operated socks, to wear while I ski. They sure help keep my feet warm when it is really cold.

Jerome has gone out with me on his snowshoes. We both take in the beauty of the mystic wonderland blanketed in snow. We watch the birds and on occasion a squirrel scampers across the snow then up a tree. We see many fox trails and know the tracks are made by our friend Foxy. During the winter Foxy red fox, comes to our place, sometimes several times a day. He enjoys the food we put out for him. He comes onto the deck, leaped onto the picnic table and eats what we put out for him. He likes bread, frosted cake, pancakes, meat and other goodies. He doesn't care for soda crackers. I put some out for him one time, he sniffed at them, picked one up and buried it in the nearby snow! When Foxy is in the woods nearby we call him and he comes running to get something to eat.

Besides Foxy we have had moose near our home. We observed a mama moose swimming in the pond. Then she climbed up on shore and was joined by a very young calf. The two disappeared into the thick woods. Another time a moose ran along the side of the house and deck and into the woods. We have seen moose tracks quite often in the driveway.

During the summer of 1998 I decided to work at a lodge, as I had done during some previous summers. Mt. McKinley Princess Lodge, only a year old, is located fifty-five miles from home. I applied there and was to start working in early May. We were having some difficulty with the muddy driveway. In the fall it was necessary to leave the pickup parked at the Igloo, along the Parks Highway, and use the four-wheeler to travel back and forth to the house. This procedure was also necessary in the early spring. To avoid having to haul all my things I wanted with me during the summer in the trailer behind the four-wheeler, we packed up the pickup ahead of time and left it parked when we needed to go from the house to the pickup on the four-wheeler.

The last weekend in April, Jerome's two daughters, their husbands and Jerome's two granddaughters came to visit. When Hally, Mike, Little Hazel and Alice arrived at the Igloo Mike called to let Jerome know they had arrived. Jerome, on his four-wheeler pulling a small trailer headed out to get them. He arrived back about an hour later with excited passengers.

The little girls were most anxious to get to Grandpa and Grandmas. Later the same day Jay and Sally arrived and the process was repeated. All this was done in reverse a few days later when our guest had to leave. The day Jay and Sally left was a bright sunny day. The following morning we were greeted by two feet of new snow. When Hally, Mike and the girls were taken out to their car, they rode covered up with a green tarp in the trailer. The girls squealed with delight to have such an exciting ride, of course Grandpa enjoyed it too.

Chapter 24

The storm lasted nine days dumping winters last big load of snow for the season. The summer was a wet rainy one. the driveway remained wet, muddy and full of ruts. Jerome named it " Many Lakes Boulevard."

Jerome took me to the lodge May 4, to where I would be living in employee housing for the summer. I had one day a week off and did manage to get home for that day. Often times Jerome came and got me or I rode the Parks Highway summer shuttle bus to the Igloo where he would pick me up. Most of the snow was gone by mid-June and the frost was going out so it was possible to drive on the road leading into our place.

Joe and Amanda were married, by Tom, April 29. Comments later expressed that it was a beautiful, very happy wedding. Having their friend perform the ceremony made it extra special.

Tragically May 25, less than a month after their marriage, Joe, Amanda along with Joe's little brother, Evan drowned at

Chena Lakes, north east of Fairbanks. They were camping and fishing during Memorial Day weekend. It was believed a grizzly bear startled them, scared them into the water, stalked them, not allowing them to get out of the water. There was evidence of a bear being there, their personal items revealed marks of being chewed by a bear, as well as bear tracks. The bear was believed to be the same bear that was seen in the area after the tragedy. Joe was 21, Amanda 18, and Evan 7. It was just the week previous that Amanda had gone bear hunting with her dad and shot her first black bear on May 21. Tom had that special bond with his dear friends, that will always remain with him.

When we looked at our wedding picture, the one we decided to give to friends and family, we commented that it was too bad that there was some other people in our picture. Those other people are Joe and Amanda--that makes our picture even more special now.

On the fourth of July my supervisor gave me an extra day off so I could attend Jerome's Moms 92nd birthday party in Big Lake, Alaska. I had the day previous off also so it made it nice to have extra time.

This corresponded with some company we were getting. My friends Marie and Ed Shelstad from Alexandria, Minnesota had sent me a letter in which Marie asked if during the summer some friends of theirs, Don and Madelyn Hale, could visit us? They would be traveling to Alaska and be in our area about the third of July.

Plans were made for them to be at our place July 3. I had talked with Madelyn on the phone once to set the final plans. We had not met these people and were anxious to have some new friends.

We met them at the Igloo, this was a common meeting place for visitors who did not know exactly how to get to our house. There is a security gate at the end of the road so it is necessary to escort those in who do not know the combination. They followed us in their motor home, parking it and joining us at our home.

We had a most enjoyable time visiting and getting acquainted. We invited them to come back and visit us again whenever they come back to Alaska.

On the morning of July 4, the Hales left to continue on their Alaskan travels. Jerome and I went to his Mom's birthday party.

At the end of July, Jerome picked fireweed flowers for jelly. I started to make it but ran out of time. After Jerome returned me to work he went back home and finished the jelly. It turned out really good.

At 6:00 A.M. August 1, 1998 as we were leaving home for me to go back to work, Jerome noticed a hawk sitting low in a tree near the house. We got our cameras, then discovered the hawk was pursuing Reddy Squirrel, he was stalking him for his breakfast.

We proceeded to take pictures, me with the video camera, Jerome taking still pictures. The hawk was oblivious to our presence, he was intent on getting the squirrel. We got quite close to the tree to watch the pursuit. Reddy would run up the tree, the hawk would dive at the squirrel, miss, then settle on a branch. This went on for about fifteen minutes, the squirrel finally got away, hiding in a nearby shed.

This little "red rascal," squirrel, as Jerome called him, continued to provide us with entertainment. Whenever we put seeds out for the chickadees, magpies, and camp robbers, (we feed all alike), the squirrel would run and chase them away, he thought. The magpies would fly straight up as Reddy ran toward them. Then when he left the birds would settle back down again to eat. This would continue as long as their was food for them to eat, sometimes the squirrel would stop to eat too. As we carefully watched the birds, we observed that all got plenty to eat, they would take turns at eating. The magpies especially liked the nugget dog food while the other birds and the squirrel ate seeds.

One afternoon in August 1998, Jerome was hand-feeding a camp robber, and Reddy Squirrel didn't like the attention being given to the birds. He climbed a tree next to the deck and chewed off the cones from a spruce tree by the house dropping them down by us as if to say, "Pay attention to me!" He chattered loudly while dropping the cones. This was a comical event and I did get some good videos of the action.

We have had a raven land on our deck a time or two, but generally they do not come around. We notice the ravens along the highway whenever we are traveling. The ravens keep a close vigilance out for scraps of "goodies" along the roads. In towns they are plentiful and can be a nuisance. We enjoy watching them as they eat and sometimes bury their food in nearby snow and sometimes a short time later retrieve it and eat. One time when we were in Fairbanks and had purchased a large bag of dog food, which we put out for our wild critters, Jerome had put it in the back of the pickup. We were in a cafe eating when I heard a conversation between two men about the green and white pickup with the bag of dog food in the back, and that the ravens were having a great time. I quickly told Jerome that the ravens were into the dog food. He went out to check to see what they were doing. When he came back he told me that the ravens had torn open the bag and were eating the dog food. He did not have anything to cover the torn bag so he laid the spare tire on it, this protected it until we got home.

My roommate at Mt. McKinley Princess Lodge was Bobbie Fitch from Florida. We have remained in contact since rooming together. While we were at the lodge we did not spend much time together, our work and schedules were not conducive for doing things together. We had different days off, she worked in the office, I was in housekeeping. She returned for the 1999 summer season, I did not. I had hoped to see her during the summer, but it was not possible.

That summer was her first time in Alaska. I enjoyed telling her about my life in Alaska. We had hoped she could visit our home sometime during the summer of 1999, but it wasn't possible. We will continue to correspond and hope to see each other some time.

Chapter 25

I spent October, 1998 in Minnesota visiting family and friends. I decided to go when there would not be a danger of bad winter weather to keep me from traveling around the state to visit. I had a very nice visit with family and many close friends.

While I was gone there was a different bear hanging around our house. Jerome tried to scare it off. He shot into the air above the bear's head however nothing was going to deter this black bear. He was becoming a pest and there was a danger of the bear causing damage or harm to someone. After several days of unsuccessful deterrence, Jerome reluctantly shot the bear. Jerome gave the bear to a friend who butchered it and processed it to eat. We had two roasts from the bear. Bear meat is quite good.

Earlier in August, on the last day of moose hunting season, Jerome helped two different friends at different times get their moose meat out from the woods after it had been shot.

From one of the moose Jerome received a quarter of the meat. He bought a pressure canner and canned 52 pints of moose meat. This is also very good meat, it was a nice treat when I returned home to have all that moose meat canned. It will last us for a couple of years.

We were given some frozen moose meat from the other friend that Jerome helped with his moose, again it was very good. We prefer wild game meat to domestic meats.

Once again I started my winter skiing, which I truly enjoy. November 17, I had gone out on the pond on my skis to take a picture of the sunset. In my haste I didn't put a coat or gloves on. I lost my balance and fell in the snow, but got my picture. When I returned to the yard I left my skis and ski poles beside the house in the snow, not standing against the house as I usually had. I was wet and cold and wanted to quickly get into the house.

The next day I went outside to go skiing, one ski pole was missing. Puzzled by this, I asked Jerome if he knew where my ski pole was? He did not. We searched for it in the yard and did not find it. Again, the next day we looked for it. Jerome found it about 50 feet from the house. He picked it up and said, "By Jove, the strap is gone."

We soon figured out our friend Foxy had taken it and chewed off the leather hand strap. After that, I kept the poles and my skis hanging on a nail in a tree by the house.

Foxy often came on the deck to eat. He most frequently came during the night. One night we could hear him on the deck. So I got up and looked out the bedroom door window. There Foxy sat on the corner of the deck bench-railing, then he began to bark. That was the only time we ever heard him bark. It was neat to hear the shrill bark of the fox.

Once again Jerome got our Christmas tree from the woods. We had a good time decorating it. This tree was quite a bit larger than the one the year before. We were a little short on ornaments, so Jerome proceeded to hang all kinds of items on the tree, stuffed animals, cookie cutters, and lastly, he hung his red-handled pliers. I asked him why he hung them on the tree? He said, "They are red aren't they? red for Christmas."

The people who previously owned our home made small wooden items such as towel racks, key racks, desk thermometers, all in the Alaska theme, animal shaped cutouts, to be sold in gift stores. They left a great deal of the unfinished items here when Jerome bought the place. Jerome and I sanded, assembled, wood burned names on, and stained these items for Christmas gifts, most were gifts to Minnesota. We have enough to do this in coming years for gifts.

By Christmas time we had nearly five feet of snow. When it was plowed our driveway was like driving in a tunnel. The trees were heavy laden with sparkling snow the wind had not removed yet. We had very little wind so the trees stayed snowy most of the time.

Christmas Eve was a gorgeous day, about 10 degrees F, from home all the way to Fairbanks. We often comment, that those who visit Alaska during the summer miss Alaskan's spectacular winter beauty. The sky was clear bordered with white mountains perforating the sky line. We marveled at the view as we traveled, it was nearly noon as we neared Fairbanks. The sun shining on the high embankment along the road, resulted in a rich alpenglow upon the snow. The sun was skirting the horizon on its way to setting in about two hours.

Our trip to Fairbanks was to get Tom for Christmas. At that time he was having vehicle problems, so he couldn't drive to our home.

We had a good time playing games and watching videos. He also went snowmobiling with Dale Koppenberg. The time went all too fast and he had to return to Fairbanks to work.

Snow on bird feeder, March 6, 1998

Chapter 26

New Year's Day we were planning to go to Big Lake, Palmer, and Wasilla to visit family and friends. New Years Eve day we went to Cantwell to get our mail.

On our way, a few miles before Cantwell, we saw two ptarmigan lying on the road. We commented on them and decided to pick them up on the way back and take them home for Foxy. We got our mail and mailed some letters. It was about a half hour later that we headed back home. When came back to the birds Jerome stopped and picked up the dead birds.

I had never seen a ptarmigan up close, so I asked to see them, Jerome handed me one. When I took it I felt that it was still warm, even with temperatures well below zero the birds were still warm. They must have been hit just ahead of us on our way into Cantwell.

I said, "Foxy, nothing we'll have them for supper!"

Jerome cleaned them and we had roasted ptarmigan, road kill for our New Year's Eve supper!

Chapter 27

On our way back home from visiting, we saw a mirage. In the sky in front of us it looked like a huge skyline of tall skyscraper buildings. This lasted for a very short time, probably less than a minute. I had never seen a mirage before. I believe only those who have witnessed such a phenomena can truly believe in such a thing. I wished I could have gotten a picture of it. I did not have time to even consider taking a picture, I was awe struck by the sight. Perhaps a picture would not turn out, I don't know.

With the holidays past and visiting done, we settled back into our lives at home. We had projects to get done. Jerome was still working on his brother's house. When he got caught up he made the beautiful mirrored cabinet for above the bathroom sink. He also made ten beautiful picture frames. These projects we refer to as "honey-do" projects, it seem as though I can always find something for my honey to do.

Our home is often filled with the aroma of beans or soup cooking on the oil stove. When we want beans for the next day

Jerome will put the ingredients together in a big cast iron kettle and put it on the oil stove. It cooks all night and the next day, by supper time we have a delicious meal accompanied with home made bread. I do all my baking in the roaster oven. We do not buy bread or bakery items, we do not have any quick box meals, I do all of the cooking the assemble method, putting it together myself, with the exception of macaroni and cheese. Soup is also made the night before the day we eat it, it too cooks all night on the oil stove.

When we shop we buy large quantities of supplies, including, usually six twenty-five pound sacks of flour. We shop to last for several months, with infrequent trips to town it is necessary to have an adequate supply on hand.

Leftovers are gladly eaten by our wild critters and birds. The birds are quite tame, we have chickadees, grosbeaks and camp robbers that eat from our hand. We do not have any dogs or cats, we are not pet people. We treasure our wild animal friends. If we had a dog or cat lurking around we would not have these friendly little wild critters. Jerome has even fed the fox from his hand. There are several fox and they stay on the deck near the picnic table where we put food out for them. We hate to think what would happen to these critters with a dog around. These creatures give us hours of entertainment with their antics. Often we can tell one bird from the other by their mannerisms and routine.

We have affectionately named our little friends. Our favorite bird is Papa Pretty Bird, the male grosbeaks. He sings cheerfully and talks bird talk as he is eating from our hand. One in particular has a routine to get me to feed him. He will sit on a round outside thermometer by the window, as he looks into the window. As I watch him he stretches his neck and chirps, begging me to feed him. If I am sitting in the chair facing the window he will fly from the thermometer to just the edge of the window watching to see if I get up. If I don't, he goes back to the thermometer and repeats this routine until I get up and feed

134

him. He then flies around the house to a window I open and feed him out of my hand. Sometimes another papa will challenge him for food as well as Mama Pretty Bird, she too will eat out of our hand. When the birds have a dispute over the food they fly beak to beak in combat straight up in the air squawking at each other, this is funny to watch. They do not carry their food off, but eat it as they sit in our hand or the feeders.

Often times when we are outside Papa Pretty Bird will fly to us and sit on our shoulder, head or arm. We then gently remove him and place him on the wind chime hanging near the door before we enter the house. He will also land on the handlebars or rack of the four-wheeler when it is being driven.

We feed them all equally and marvel at their individual elegant design. The magpies are especially elegant-looking in their white, black and deep blue coloring. They carry their food off and stow it in nearby trees, or clumps of snow among the branches. Their favorite food is nugget dog food. Along with our supplies we purchase large bags of dog food as well as sunflower seeds for the birds.

Chickadees always fly away with their seeds. They too eat out of the peanut butter feeders that Jerome made. We have them hanging in front of the windows. The camp robbers too carry their food off and stow it in nearby trees. I believe what falls to the ground is found by mice, weasels or Reddy Squirrel, so all the critters are well fed.

Mr. Magpie and Mr. Fox, February 5, 1999

Mr. Fox getting his sandwich, March 14, 1999

Foxy posing, April 7, 1999

Chapter 28

At the senior luncheon in Cantwell, we met Bob and Pam Gilbertson, owners of the Backwoods Lodge in Cantwell, as well as Bernd and Susan Richter, their assistant managers. At one of these luncheons Bernd and I had a conversation about my working at Mt. McKinley Princess Lodge. He mentioned Backwoods Lodge may need a housekeeper for the summer season.

I contemplated the idea of possibly working at Backwoods Lodge that next summer season of 1999. Jerome and I discussed the preference to working in Cantwell over returning to Mt. McKinley Princess. It would not be practical to drive to Cantwell each day, we have only one vehicle. Jerome would need the pickup for his carpenter work he would be doing near the park entrance.

I called Bob and expressed my interest in working at his lodge. He told me in a month or so he would have things figured out and let me know. The next time we talked, Bob asked me to come to the lodge to do the paper work. I was told the duties of the housekeeping work. He also told me there was a fifth-wheeler camper in a wooded area near the lodge that would provide living quarters for me. I was hired and was scheduled to start working May 15, 1999.

Jerome was still working near the Park entrance. New buildings were being built to accommodate more Alaskan visitors during the upcoming summer season. Prior to my moving to Cantwell for the summer, Jerome moved most of my things to the camper. He did this early so he could haul them in the pickup before the driveway became too muddy for travel. He did this on his way to work, at that time he was working about 42 miles from home. His work there was completed in time for a short break before he started another building project.

February 23, 1999 we stopped to talk with our friends Clayton and Erika Flagg while shopping in a Fairbanks store. During conversation Clayton and Erika asked Jerome and I to come to their place for supper some night. Later that week Clayton called Jerome and asked him if he would build their new house for them? This was really a surprise. Jerome agreed to get together with them and talk about it. They lived at mile 229 Parks Highway. (Mile markings are often used to tell where a place is located because there are no other means to describe a location.)

I had met Clayton in 1994 while working at Kantishna Roadhouse. That summer Erika Rothenbuhler from Switzerland worked at the roadhouse for a couple months before returning to Switzerland. She and Clayton did not start seeing each other until Erika returned a couple years later. They were married by Bruce Burnell at the Burnell home in the Alaska Range Mountains, February 22, 1998. Ray Atkins did the flying for those who went out for the wedding, including Erika's parents from Switzerland.

Jerome knew Clayton from the summer of 1993 at Kantishna Roadhouse, the summer Jerome did the log work on the new lodge building. He did not know Erika, however.

Plans were started for Jerome to build their house. After he got their basic idea of what they wanted, he drew up the blue prints, a process that took him three weeks to do, working on it nearly every day. As he sat at the table with paper, pencil, and measuring tools, I made a conscious effort not to talk to him. This was my decision not his request, I did not want to disturb his work.

The building project would probably last until mid-October. He would need to drive about 40 miles from home to the building site. It worked out quite well, because he could stay with me most of the time while I was at the lodge. By staying with me he saved 50 miles a day traveling distance. He did need to go home once in a while to get tools and water my plants.

When I was hired at Backwoods I was the only housekeeper at that time, with another one probably being hired. After thinking about it, I offered to work seven days a week. As long as I was at the lodge, without a vehicle, what would I do on my days off? I may as well work, but that did created a very long summer.

Susan and Bernd had been at the lodge for four years and planned to expand their children's book writing and Alaskan crafts they were already doing, so they would no longer be assistant managers. To date they have written *"When Grandma Visited Alaska She...," "When Grandma and Grandpa Visited Alaska they...," "Do Alaskans Live in Igloos?", "Uncover Alaskan's Wonders," "How Alaska Got Its Flag," and "Peek-A-Boo Alaska."*

We became friends as well as co-workers. I was toying with the idea of making a calendar with some pictures I have taken in Alaska. Bernd was looking at my pictures one day and suggested I write a book. I thought about it for about ten seconds and said, "That would be fun."

Summer at Backwoods proved to be interesting. I met

139

people from many different places. One experience involved an older couple from Maryland. They stayed at the lodge for nine days. One day I observed this couple leaning down and scurrying around the walkway near their door. This activity puzzled me, I walked over to them and said, "What are you doing?" Lorna said, "I got it," to her husband Herbert. By that time I was beside them. She said she was catching a spider, I asked her, "did you get it?"

What do you mean, "did I get it?" As she held up her hand, index finger and thumb together, she was holding a tiny spider. Quickly Herb had gone into their room and emerged with a small clear container, Lorna dropped the spider into it. Herb explained that he caught and studied spiders, he did this for a museum in Maryland. He said he had a special permit to catch spiders in Denali National Park.

The next day while I was working I found a spider. I quickly put it in a paper cup, folding it shut to save for Herb. Later that day I gave the spider to Herb. Later I checked back on my spider. Herb had put it in a small vial and fed it a mosquito. He told me he would take the spider back home to the museum, enter it in a display and label it as being from Backwoods Lodge, Cantwell, Alaska. Well now I would have a special spider in a museum, how many people can lay claim to such fame?

Chapter 29

Jerome picked me up after I had finished working on July 11. This was my first night home since I had started working. I was tired and anxious to be at home until the next morning when I would have to return to work.

When we got home I said I would wash the dishes. Jerome told me after his shower he would do the dishes and make supper. So I just sat in my recliner enjoying resting.

Jerome had finished the dishes and was cleaning carrots for a roast he was making for supper. We were engaged in conversation when I heard what I thought was an engine stop. I commented on it, Jerome said it was probably a train stopping at the siding across Colorado Lake. I hadn't been home for a while and was not used to the train sounds, we continued talking.

Suddenly there was a knock at the door. Jerome said, "Oh that's probably Steve, he is in a tent across the lake, and comes over for water."

I went to the door, opened it and looked at a man wearing waders and wondered, did he walk across the lake?! Looking at the man I said, "Are you Steve?"

He looked bewildered and said, "No, I am not, I am Jim, Jim Borden."

I said, "Come on in anyway." He came into the house and told us he was flying to Fairbanks and became socked in by bad weather. He had flown a few miles beyond us and saw a lake with some cabins, but he didn't see any activity. He needed to use a telephone and didn't think there was one there. So he flew back to the lake by us. He said he saw lights on on the outside of the house, so he decided to land in the lake. He also told us after he landed he heard the generator running and saw a pickup in the yard so he was hopeful someone was around.

Ah Ha!! The engine I had heard stop was the airplane when it landed by our place!

Jim made his call to Fairbanks explaining his situation to someone he was to see that day and that he couldn't get there.

Jim told us he was a surgeon and lived in Soldotna, Alaska. He said his wife was out in the plane. We told him to bring her in. He said he couldn't fly any further and that they had camping equipment and if it was all right with us they could camp on the lake shore. Then, perhaps, the next day they could fly out.

On the way out to the plane Jerome and I quickly discussed the fact that they might as well stay in our house, we had a guest room. At the plane we met Eileen, Jim's wife. Jerome and Jim secured the plane using the place that had been used by our previous home owner, to secure their plane.

We all went into the house and quickly became acquainted. We learned that Eileen too was a doctor, she has her practice in Soldotna, where they live.

By this time it was nearly 7:00 P.M. and supper was done. Jerome asked them to eat with us. We all enjoyed his moose roast he had made, along with home made bread I had previously made at the camper and froze to keep it fresh. I brought it home that day.

We asked them to spend the night in the house instead of camping out, they graciously accepted. During conversation it was revealed that Jim and Jerome knew some of the same people, some in Cordova, Alaska as well as another place. Jim was talking about an Ed King, in Cordova. Well we were surprised. I quickly got up reached up by the window trim and retrieved a blue business card. I showed it to Jim. The card was one Ed had sent saying that his business was feeding birds in a feeding pond, now that he is retired. The card had a picture of Ed on it feeding birds. This was quite a coincidence. Jim also told us he knew Ray Atkins from Cantwell. We told him we also knew him. He then told us about meeting Ray quite a few years ago.

Eileen and I discovered that we both have some of the same books, a fishing chart, and interests alike. We also recommended books to each other to read. We talked about one of our favorite authors, Patrick McManus. Eileen said they too had a McManus book and really enjoyed it.

Eileen washed the dishes as we enjoyed lively conversation. It wasn't but a short time and it seemed like they were long-time friends who had come to visit. We talked until about 11:30 P.M. Jim told us that the next day, July 12, was their second wedding anniversary. They were married on a boat near Dutch Harbor, Alaska near the end of the Aleutian Islands. They were married by the boat captain. This was ironic because our second wedding anniversary was just a month before, June 13.

Before we retired for the night Jim said, "I'll make breakfast for you in the morning, I have some eggs and reindeer sausage in the plane I'll go get."

They went out and brought in the things for breakfast as well as what they needed for the night and the next morning. When we settled down for the night, it was nearly midnight.

143

At 6:00 A.M. we were all up and anxious for the day. Jim made us eggs, reindeer sausage with bagels, which was a delicious breakfast. Eileen once again did the dishes. Jim made phone calls trying to get an aviation weather report. He also attempted to call Ray Atkins but he was not at home.

They decided to try and leave. We went out and bid them good bye, with the promise we would see each other again. They took off, circled the lake above us a few times then came back. Jim said the weather was not suitable for flying. He said, "I want to be able to fly again," not wanting to take a risk that may be his last. It isn't wise when flying conditions are undesirable.

We left our new friends when Jerome took me back to the lodge to work. We told them they could stay as long as they wanted. They successfully took off around 10:00 A.M. That truly was the highlight of our summer.

Jim and Eileen Borden landing on Colorado Lake, July 12, 1999

Chapter 30

On July 16 was the ninetieth birthday party for George Goble. His wife, family, and friends prepared a big party for him. Nearly the entire community of Cantwell was there, about 100 people, that included some people that did not live in the area. We all had a good time helping George celebrate his birthday.

Jerome helped me with my work one day when we did not have very many guests checking out. We finished about 11:00 A.M., left and went to Fairbanks. We returned from Fairbanks getting back to the camper at the lodge about 1:00 A.M. the next morning. Jerome needed to go on home to unload some items we had purchased in Fairbanks. At that time the Igloo was still open. Jerome stopped there about 1:30 A.M.. He later related this story to me. Joni Costello was working there. She told Jerome that two men had just been in there and asked her where the river was. She questioned them as to why, and what river they were referring to. Well, they told her that they had put two of their friends in a canoe and were suppose to pick them up.

She asked them where that was? They replied, "Talkeetna." She was really surprised because Talkeetna was well over a hundred miles from there. She said they left headed north! That is a direction in which a river generally does not flow. There are many rivers so it was not known which one the men were talking about.

We have talked about this incident and wonder if those men ever found their friends, and if they did where and when? One sure thing--those canoeist most certainly had a true Alaskan Experience!!

On the evening of July 25, Jerome and I were reading in the camper when we heard a vehicle. I looked out the window, but didn't recognize who it was. Jerome went out to inquire as to what they wanted. A man got out of the truck and told Jerome he had just seen a grizzly bear in the woods headed towards our camper.

I called Bob and told him about the bear. Pam called the guests to warn them that there was a bear in the area. Bob came out with his rifle in case the bear was to cause any harm. The two men in the truck left, Jerome and I got into our pickup and drove around, but did not see the bear. There were three teenagers walking on the road, so we gave them a ride home, in case the bear was nearby.

Less that a week later a neighbor called Bob and told him he had seen a grizzly in the driveway of the lodge. Again we did not see it. A large grizzly had been seen around the area for several weeks prior to these episodes, perhaps the same one.

On August 2, Jerome and I went home in the evening to water my plants and check on things. The couple of times I was home I got to watch the pair of loons that had a nest on the island in the pond. They had two little ones hatch. It was fun to watch them swim around the pond. On the edge of the pond there was a sea gull with one little one. Only it wasn't so little, it was a gray-brown color. It did not get food for itself, but waited for its parent to bring food and feed it. These birds were interesting to watch. On our way back, at the end of our driveway, we saw a grizzly sow and a cub running along the road. I missed getting a picture of them.

Jerome was home a few days before actually starting the log work on the Flagg's house. I called him each evening from the lodge. I attempted to call him several nights in a row, without success, I was sure he was at home. I called the Igloo to see if he had been there. I asked Joni, who was working there, if she had seen Jerome. I explained that I was attempting to call him and was becoming concerned.

Joni made some calls to find out what the problem was. Jay Holmberg called me to inform me that a bear had chewed into the phone wire pedestal not to far from our place. There is some type of wax that is used inside of the pedestal box on the joint connectors, and may have been what the bear was trying to get. Joni had talked to Jay and in turn he called me. In the meantime Jerome called me wondering why I had not called him. He could call out and was not aware that he could not receive incoming calls.

On August 1, Gale and I took about an hour from work to attend a barbecue with all the fixings, at the state trooper's residence, less than a mile from the lodge. The local State Trooper, Sonny Sabala, his wife Jo, and their family put on a barbecue each summer for the local people. I was really impressed that the State Trooper would do this. How many people can say their state trooper had a neighborhood barbecue? The barbecue lasted all afternoon with many of the local people attending and enjoying a good social time as well as good food.

One day while I was working I saw a weasel running along the walkway in front of the guest rooms. I watched for a minute and then saw another weasel appear. I watched their antics, dodging around on the walkway. I got my camera, which I always kept on my supply cart, and took four pictures of them as they ran and played. They ran around on my supply

147

cart. They also ran in and out of an opening under the walkway. Their movements were so quick I could hardly keep track of them. Then the third one appeared wanting to join in the fun. Just as quickly as they appeared they were gone and did not come back. A guest was lucky enough to take pictures of them too.

Backwoods Lodge had a resident mama moose that was often seen. I looked out the window of the camper and saw a small baby moose behind the dumpster. I got my camera and went outside to take a picture of it. As I started out around the trees I suddenly noticed mama moose standing with her back end toward me. I stopped in my tracks. She turned, looked at me and crossed the driveway toward her baby. I got a good side picture of her but not her baby. I had lost view of it in the woods.

Mama Moose at Backwoods Lodge, Cantwell,
August 17, 1999

Chapter 31

At the end of my summer work season I returned back home. I had spent only two nights at home since May. It was nice to be back home. I had worked 106 consecutive days, became ill with a cold and missed three days of work. The owners and other employees, Gale Andersen and Susan who did office work as well as the laundry and other tasks, and Bernd pitched in and did my work for those three days. I then worked another week, during that time Gabe Kehn and Beth Lynn, from Idaho were hired as the new assistant managers. I assisted Beth and Gabe in learning the housekeeping part of the lodge; they caught on very quickly. They are looking forward to their first winter in Alaska.

Jerome now had to drive to his house building site from home adding 50 miles each day. This would be for probably only another month or so.

On September 11 we received a phone call from the State Trooper asking us if we would like to have some moose meat.

Jerome had just gotten home from work and was tired. With a little encouragement from me, while he was still on the phone, he said we would be there in about an hour.

Jerome and I went to Cantwell to the State Troopers building and were met by trooper Sonny Sabala and Brian Stevenson of Fish and Wildlife. We were given the moose meat and returned home, where Jerome and I cut and wrapped the meat. This moose had been obtained by the state officials. When we were taking care of the meat we found three bullet holes in the moose. While I was eating some of the moose later in the fall, (during one of our candle light suppers, I bit into a bullet fragment). We were not told about the whereabouts the moose came from. We appreciated the delicious meat.

Chapter 32

September 16 I went to work with Jerome, later that day he took me to the Park entrance where I caught the shuttle bus to Fairbanks. Tom met me at the Visitors Center in Fairbanks. I spent the week visiting my friend Roni as well as with my friend Shaun. Tom and I spent a great deal of time together, shopping, going out to eat, to the movies and of course mud bogging on the mud flats south of Fairbanks. He now had a 1976 Jeep. I guess boys never tire of playing in the mud. This wasn't quite a repeat of the mud bogging we did that day in May of 1997, but it was fun and we talked about that day .

Tom's girlfriend, Sandy Johnson, was a frequent visitor. She is from the small village of Galena, Alaska, 240 air miles west of Fairbanks. Galena is not accessible by roads. Sandy is attending UAF and will graduate next year with the same degree I earned at the university. Sandy has had some of the same teachers I did. I enjoyed the time I spent with her.

Jerome finished with the Flagg home on October 14,

151

1999. I had asked him when he had started in the spring when he thought he would finish building the house. He said, "Oh, probably about the middle of October." Well, he was pretty close on his guess.

The house is 55 feet by 20 feet with the back section being a shop for Clayton to do his craft projects. There is one bedroom, and is built to add more. This bedroom is the only room on the second level and is located in the center of the building. The home does not have a well but a 1,000 gallon holding tank for water storage. They get water from the nearby community center and haul it in a tank in the back of their pickup, then pump it into the storage tank. It would be too expensive to have a well dug. Water is not that good in that area and is very deep, so it was not practical to have a well dug. Their new home has a bathroom, septic system, and electricity.

Clayton makes beautiful wooden jewelry boxes, clocks using caribou antlers, as well as beautiful earrings. He is very talented, producing excellent quality work. He has his items for sale at the Goose Lake Studio in Denali, Camp Denali during the summer and Artworks in Fairbanks year round. He makes things for special orders also.

Erika also does lovely work. She does screen painting on scarves as well as pictures. She too sells her items at the Goose Lake Studio during the summer and Artworks in Fairbanks year round. Both Erika and Clayton are fortunate to be so very talented.

When Clayton would tell someone he was having a new house built, he would say, "It is going to be built by--," whoever he was telling would say, "By Jerome, the best." That person seemed to know who the carpenter would be. Jerome is excellent at building and an expert log man.

In September 1951 Jerome was featured and pictured in a book, *Where else but ALASKA?* by Sara and Fred Machetanz. He helped build their new log home near Palmer, Alaska. He is cited as, "perhaps the finest axe man I've ever seen. Ought to be--been at it since before he was long as an axe handle..." as stated by Jerome's dad. He has since lived up to that reputation. Jerome is mentioned in another book, *Log Cabins of Alaska*, by Harry W. Walker. It is a 1999 book featuring log cabins in Alaska. It tells about Jerome's log work on the Kantishna Roadhouse.

In the 1960s Jerome lived in Cordova, Alaska, and worked in a boat shop. There he worked on skiffs and repaired boats with his partner Bud Banta. He has house boat plans and house plans he has made as his "someday" projects. He has built ten log homes.

Jerome's work on his brother's house continued for over two years. He also built their garage. Carpenter work is not his only special talent, he also has made gold nugget jewelry to sell.

Clayton and Erika's house, September 16, 1999

Clayton and Erika and Jerome on porch of completed home, November 18, 1999

Chapter 33

The seasons change from summers lush green to the brilliant colors of fall, toward the spectacular glory of winter. In the pond in front of our home I have watched the summer as it gives way to winter. The once dark stone covered mountains reflected in the often mirrored water of the pond, now look back in the stark contrast of white.

Along the driveway the bushes were iced with the drizzle of snow frosting looking like a frosted cookie. This thin icing permitted the darkened plants to peek through as if to resist the sure-to-come heavy snow.

I pondered over the past six years I have lived in Alaska, asking myself, "why wouldn't I want to live in Alaska? It is truly the most fascinating place I have ever been."

One early evening in October 1999 I walked down our driveway, as I often do, to meet Jerome on his way home from working on the house he was building.

Stopping on the top of the hill about one half mile from

home, I was taken by my awesome surroundings. Standing in the road, I slowly turned completely around marveling at the splendor.

My immediate surrounding were spruce trees, dark green, tall and silent. The grasses were brown and thin, looking as though their frail structure would break at the slightest breeze. Leaves from the trees were gone, flowers gone, the greenery of the bushes all gone. All this in preparation for the next season, waiting for the soft silent blanket of white to cover their bareness, left after summers burst of beauty.

In the distance a squirrel chattered to let me know he was about. A bird flew up from the hidden bushes. They broke the silence, however, briefly.

As I continued to turn, looking beyond my adjacent tranquility, I saw dazzling white mountains completely encompassing my world, my eyes drinking in the beauty. Beyond the white peaks jutting into the sky, the sky was lit with pale peach-pink. The colors softly changed to a bright tangerine, where the sun bid farewell to a beautiful October day, as it slipped behind the magnificence of Mt. McKinley. I didn't need to wonder -- *"Why would Grandma move to Alaska."*

Talkeetna Mountains reflected in pond in front of our home, October 3, 1999

156

Chapter 34

It was October 16th Jerome and I attended the funeral of Buster Barnhardt, a long time friend of Jerome's. That morning we had planned on leaving about 8:00 A.M. When Jerome went out to start the pickup he noticed that there was a flat tire. He proceeded to get the air compressor and some tire plugs to repair the tire. He put on some coveralls to protect his good clothes while working on the tire, as well as changing from his good shoes to boots. When he was putting the air compressor away, a wheel fell off before he got back to the shop. So he left it set in the yard. It was nearly 9:00 A.M. when we left the house. Jerome commented that we probably should have left at 7:00 A.M. I counted the hours between 7:00 A.M. and 1:00 P.M., that was six hours and it only took about three hours to get to Palmer. About a mile down our driveway I looked down at Jerome's feet and said, "I think we better go back so you can change your boots for your dress shoes." So he turned around and went back home to change his footwear. We reached

157

Wasilla a little before 11:00 A.M. Jerome wanted to stop at the bank. The bank was closed. We drove on to Palmer. There we went to the bank parking lot and saw that the bank would be open at 12:00 noon. It was 11:30 A.M. I thought perhaps we would wait the half hour for the bank to open, but Jerome said, "We had better go or we will be late." I said, "Late for what?" He said, the funeral, that's what we came here for". I was puzzled and said, "The funeral is at 1:00 P.M". Jerome thought for a second or two then said he had gotten mixed up on the time. He had talked to someone else who had to be in Palmer the same day at 11:00 A.M. He had mixed up the two times. During our trip I noticed that Jerome seemed to be in a hurry. We often stop to eat or for a break when traveling, but that time we didn't. I couldn't understand the rush.

Jerome decided to check to see how the repaired tire was holding up. He discovered that the repair plug was starting to come out. We drove to several locations trying to find someone who would change the tire. The repair shops were either closed or booked up until the next Tuesday! Finely we found a place that, even though was very busy with people waiting, agreed to change the tire when we explained our dilemma. The tire was changed and we got to the church a little after 12:30 P.M. (in plenty of time.) As it turned out, all the hurrying had been necessary or we would have been late. Buster had a great sense of humor. I like to think that he was watching down on us during our comical escapade and smiling.

Chapter 35

During early fall a red breasted nuthatch joined our other birds. It spends every day from daylight to dark, carrying one sunflower seed off at a time. It flies to the trees or a nearby bush with the seed it has taken from the bird feeder.

Jerome and I talked about how hard poor little Nutty works to carry seeds away. Perhaps these seeds will be eaten by other birds, squirrels, mice, and small critters of the woods. Nutty will probably find few if any if he searches for them.

Looking in our bird book we learned that this type of nuthatch is one listed as "casual or accidental," in our area. We had not seen any in the previous years.

Winter arrived on October 18, 1999, with two feet of snow falling in two days. Temperatures were mild, near 30 degrees F. The snow was heavy and wet, usually the snow is quite dry. With the wet snow it was possible to make a snowman. It had been many years since I had made a snowman. I rolled the snow into a base, placed the midsection, then the head. I used a carrot for its nose, black plastic pieces of a bag shaped for eyes, a red bottle lid made the mouth. I added arms using a stick with socks on the ends. The final touches were spruce cone buttons down the front, to make it look like a coat. With warm temperatures it lost its head and I had to do some reconstruction.

My first time out on skis this winter was on October 23rd a beautiful bright sunny day with a temperature of zero F, ideal skiing conditions. I make my own ski trails, being the only skier around I have the job of going through the deep snow to make a trail, but I enjoy doing this. I was only out about forty five minutes. I needed to get limbered up and used to skiing after the summer. It was great to be out in the crisp air. The snow revealed fox, squirrel, and bird tracks.

The previous night the fox had been back. It had searched all around the house, on the deck and picnic table, looking for food. I had put some food scraps out before we went to bed. We were glad to see Foxy tracks, telling us it was back.

On the night of November 3, 1999, we were in bed when I heard some noise outside. I went downstairs to see, thinking it was probably the fox. It was the fox. The next morning we looked outside through the picture window, and we saw what all the noise had been about the previous night. Jerome had wired an old large frying pan to the picnic table, which we put food in for the fox. This frying pan was gone from the table. We looked out on the snow on the pond and there was the pan. This pan is quite heavy and would not be easy for a fox to carry, but he did. I had a birdhouse setting on the picnic table too. It had a removable roof. Well, the birdhouse was gone from the table too. The fox had knocked it off the picnic table and carried the removable roof out in the snow beyond the frying pan. The lid was off the five gallon bucket, on the deck for bird food. The lid was a large kettle turned upside down over the bucket. Foxy had gotten the lid off but did not spill the food. I had put out two squash rind halves, for the birds to peck at. Well, the fox had also carried them off!

Since then, we discovered that the fox liked nugget dog food we put out for the magpies. We put it out for the fox at night when the birds are not around. We have three different fox that come and eat, taking turns, sometimes squabbling. One night the young fox was eating the dog food when the other fox appeared. That one challenged the young one and won, chasing it off the table. The young one then laid under the table whining. Another time two foxes had a dispute over the food on the picnic table. They stood on their hind legs hitting each other with their front legs. This encounter ended by one fox kicking the other one with its hind legs. There appears to be the one fox that came last year, a young one and another one that has coloring quite different than the other two. We call this one, "New Foxy", it has a black tail, black legs, black face and ears, its back is black and red mixed. This one is a cross-fox, very pretty.

One bright and sunny day I noticed about thirty small tongue marks on the picture window. As the light hit the window just right I wondered what had made those marks. I remembered seeing similar marks last spring, yes, it was Foxy who had licked the glass. He often begs for food by sitting on the picnic table looking in at us as he tilts his head back and forth as if waiting to be fed. Foxy most likely licked the window sometime when we were not around to see him.

The squirrel we now have around is a different one from the two previous winters. We can tell by its actions. It too likes to chase the birds, but doesn't really accomplish anything. The birds just come back. We enjoy watching Reddy eat out of the feeder that is placed directly on the window frame of the kitchen window. When we are at the table we have a close view of Reddy as well as the birds. It is interesting to watch the squirrel eat sunflower seeds, then stop after so many and clean his face and paws. I put lint from the clothes dryer in the feeder, Reddy likes to take it. I suppose he uses it for his nest or to insulate his house. One day after he had taken the lint, rolling it up in a tight ball in his mouth, he carried it off and returned with some pieces of yellow fiberglass insulation. Maybe he thought I wanted to trade with him.

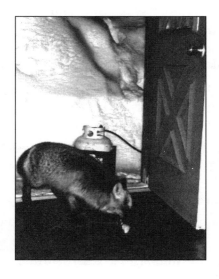

Foxy getting a treat, January 1, 2000

Chapter 36

For Thanksgiving we were invited out for dinner. It was an interesting meal. I asked Jerome, "What was that I couldn't eat, you didn't take, and Uncle Henry fed to the dog?" I am not sure what it was but, I believe it was a family tradition/speciality which requires an acquired taste!! During the meal Uncle Henry said, "I think I have to spit." Several people pointed in the direction of the bathroom, but he rose slightly then sat back down. With that, little four-year-old Allie did spit, her mouthful of cranberry sauce, not once but twice. She was trying to be persuaded by others to eat her cranberry sauce. I can't blame a four-year-old for not liking cranberry sauce when many adults do not either.

Reading continues to be one of our favorite pastime. We have about 660 books. This number is always changing as we continue to get new ones. I have given away about a dozen books. Of course Alaska books are our favorite. Sixty eight of these books are about Alaska. Probably about 200 books are paperback novels that are not all that interesting, but those books were here when Jerome bought the house. Most of the other books Jerome had and moved them to our home from Fairbanks. We often receive books for gifts.

One of my friends and former classmate, Pat Myers who lives in Fairbanks, works in the Fast Photo Shop in Fairbanks. She has developed and did reprints for me of many of the pictures that appear in this book. I remember when I first met her she told me she had lived in Cantwell in the 1970s. I didn't think about that until we were talking one day and I told her I was getting married and would be living twenty-five miles south of Cantwell. Since then I have gotten to know many of the people she knew when she lived in Cantwell.

Since I have moved to Cantwell I do not get to see some of my Fairbanks friends as often, whenever possible I enjoy meeting with the special ladies from University Baptist Church for their monthly luncheons. We also exchange Christmas cards and letters.

When we get the mail I always look forward to the *Sauk Centre Herald*, sent to me by my dear Minnesota friends Marie and Orville Vangstad.

Chapter 37

In November 1998 I took a picture of the Igloo building, which I sent to The International Library of Photography in Owen Mills, Maryland, entering it in an amateur photo contest. In August I received a letter stating that my photo, *Alaskan Igloo*, was chosen from thousands, would be one of 750 photos to appear in a coffee table book, *Voyage Through Time*. This book is due to be out in spring of 2000. Besides that I would be eligible to win a cash prize of $1,000 or $10,000, if my photo is chosen as a winning one. I was thrilled and honored to have my photo chosen for this book.

Later I received another letter from The International Library of Photography informing me that the photo *The Little House Out Back*, also been chosen for another book *Dawns Reflections*.   This picture is of the outhouse that stands in our yard, but never used.

I received another surprise from The International Library of Photography. A letter to me stated that my two pictures are on the Internet and can be found at www.picture.com then search under DeVonne Koppenberg. These photo can be bought when the appear on such items as calendars, coffee mugs, tee-shirts, and puzzles for sale by the company. I will get a percentage of all sales made using my photos.

Outhouse picture as it appears in *"Dawns Reflections"* published by The International Library of Photography. Photo taken March 5, 1998.

The igloo picture as it appears in *"Voyage Through Time"* published by The International Library of Photography. Photo taken November 18, 1998.

Chapter 38

Jerome is making us some new kitchen chairs, that he designed. He had hoped to get them done by Christmas, but it will be closer to New Year's. The chairs are a simple design but very nice. It takes a lot of work to take a piece of wood shape it and cut it and join it with other pieces to make a beautiful chair. I continue to marvel at his woodworking talent.

Jerome and I needed to go to Fairbanks for a doctor appointment on December 22. By the afternoon of the day before we received two additional feet of new snow which had fallen in a thirty-six hour period. We decided it would be wise to go to Fairbanks the afternoon before the appointment day. I took pictures of our yard, out-buildings and the pickup as Jerome was shoveling it out for our trip. It was still snowing and we wondered what it would be like when we got on the road? We left home about 3:00 P.M. It took us an hour to get to Cantwell, twenty five miles from our home. The visibility was near zero with temperatures rising to near 30 degrees F, causing slippery road conditions. As we traveled north on the Parks Highway we encountered a variety of weather conditions ranging from heavy snow, to sleet and rain. All this made driving less than desirable. Driving with extreme caution is best in that kind of weather.

When we arrived in Fairbanks five-and-a-half hours later (a trip that normally takes three hours), we noticed a considerable change in the temperature from what it had been when we were there the week of December 6th. The temperatures then were very cold, ranging from a high of -10 degrees F to a low in the -30s degrees F. Without wind the subzero temperatures are tolerable. Of course it is very important to have proper clothing and avoid having bare skin exposed for even a short time.

On our way to Fairbanks we saw a fireworks stand open. Fireworks are often used to celebrate the new year. There are several of these stands along the highway toward Anchorage too. Fireworks have always been synonymous with the fourth of July. But in Alaska fireworks can not be seen in the night sky in July. Fireworks are often shot off not for the visual but for the audio affect. On News Year's Eve there are special places that one can go to see special displays of fireworks, the same as done in other states on the fourth of July.

Arriving in Fairbanks, we saw a large bank thermometer displaying 16 degrees above zero F. The next day at noon it was a balmy 45 degrees F a drastic change from a week and a half earlier. Other parts of the state were also experiencing unusual weather. Rain caused snow to melt in the Delta area and they also had high winds of 88 mph. The little village of Northway southeast of Fairbanks set a record with a high temperature of 47 degrees F on December 22nd, the previous high recorded was 20 degrees F in 1990. There were some areas where temperatures rose rapidly, one place it rose 30 degrees F in ten minutes.

During most winters it is not unusual for a big difference

168

in temperatures between short distances. In Fairbanks it may be 20 degrees F below zero while in the hills on the outskirts of Fairbanks it may be near 30 degrees F above zero. Often there is a significant difference in temperatures a few blocks apart. This is the same for other parts of Alaska as well. Temperatures are often different just a few miles apart.

On our return trip December 22nd the sky was clear and it appeared to be a nice day, although we knew road conditions would not be the best yet in the Cantwell area. The day before was the shortest day of the year, the sun-up time was also the same on the twenty-second. As we headed out of Fairbanks, it had begun to get dark. About ninety miles down the road the moon was shining bright. I had heard on the news earlier in the week that the moon was to be brighter than ever due to some unusual conditions. It was predicted that weather conditions would be unusual with higher and lower tides as well as probably more earthquakes and volcano eruptions. This perhaps explains the unusual weather patterns we were experiencing. The roads were pretty good going to Healy. When we stopped at the Totem Inn to eat we learned that road conditions were progressively worse toward Cantwell, another forty miles, in fact the roads were closed in some places, with trucks and cars in the ditch causing injuries and damaged vehicles. We were told that there was about two inches of ice on the highway along with snow and blowing snow.

In the parking lot of the Totem Inn was parked a large motor home towing a large boat. This was a comical sight in mid-Alaska three days before Christmas. Just as strange was a ditch full of water across the highway from Totem Inn.

Jerome found out that even if we could have gotten past Cantwell to our turn-off we could not have gotten home. We decided to get a motel room at Totem Inn. Early the afternoon of December 23, we left Healy heading toward Cantwell. The sky was mostly clear with the sun low in the horizon and a few scattered clouds. With a temperature of near 0 degree F it was

169

a beautiful day. As we traveled the amount of snow on the road increased as did the wind. By the time we reached Cantwell it was white-out conditions as the strong wind swirled the fresh snow.

We got our mail and went to the Time-To-Eat Cafe to learn what we could about the roads. State trooper Sonny Sabala came in greeting everyone and said the road was open but ice-covered. A vehicle had gone into the ditch some miles south of Cantwell. We also found out that the two mile road into our place was not open and wouldn't be until about 5:00 P.M., about three hours away.

When we arrived home we learned that it had taken the plow seven hours to open the road to our house. It had been plowed on both Monday and Tuesday as well. It is done by a private plow that was kept busy. When we drove down the driveway most of the snow banks were higher that the pickup. The plowed part was a narrow opening, like driving down a snow tunnel even higher than previous winters. This additional four feet of snow is piled high in our yard and the two decks. Jerome had to shovel to the house and the steps to get inside. The snow is piled high under the windows. Some of this snow is what slid off the house roof. The deck railing is piled about five feet high blocking our view to the pond and mountains.

I got a pleasant surprise when I read my mail. I had received a letter from Mr. and Mrs. Levi from Pepperell, MA. The letter in part read:

.... "We did not get very many spiders last summer, partly because of bad weather, partly because we collected only some of our time there, but mainly, I think, because we seem to have less energy than we had 50 years ago when we first started doing this. So far, in four short visits to Alaska, we found about 80 kinds of spiders. There probably are about 200-300 different kinds in the Alaska area."

Herb is emeritus Professor of Biology at Harvard

170

University, and Curator of Arachnids and Myriapods at the Museum of Comparative Zoology (MCZ), a part of Harvard University.

"The spider you caught ended up in the collections of the MCZ. The Museum has the second largest spider collection worldwide. Specimens are loaned to qualified specialists studying taxonomy, predators of insects, spider silk, venoms, distribution, ecology or other aspects of spiders, and visitors come to the Museum from all over the world to work with the collections.

Herb studies tropical orb-weaving spiders, borrowing collections from 15-20 different museums, trying to identify the spiders, naming new kinds, and publishing guides that permit ecologists and behaviorists to figure out what animals are found in their areas.

Would you want to collect more spiders next summer? If so, we can send you vials with preserving fluid..."

They also sent me a book they have written, *SPIDERS AND THEIR KIN*. The book is quit interesting, I did not realize there was so much to know about spiders! Oh yes, I took them up on collecting spiders this next summer, hope I can be successful and find some.

Christmas time was quiet at our house. Tom had planned on spending it with us, but got sick with the flu and could not make it. We saved the Christmas presents for when he planned on coming down New Year's weekend. That did not work either, with temperatures at -55 degrees F, he was wise to stay at home. Jerome and I opened our Christmas gifts on New Years Eve.

On Tuesday before Christmas, Alaska Public Radio had a program on in which people could call in from anywhere in Alaska and extend season greetings to family and friends in other parts of the state. With it often being difficult to travel to be with family, this provided a service for these special greetings. Many calls came from Barrow greeting those in

Anchorage as well as other places. It was interesting to listen to, especially when these messages were spoken in the native Eskimo language.

Jerome has been busy plowing snow. He spent five hours plowing day before yesterday, five hours again yesterday. I asked him when he came in last night how far he had gotten? He said, "Well, I can't tell where I am at because the snow is so high on each side of the road." He is back at it again today, the last day of my entry in this book which brings it up to News Year's Eve.

We went to Clayton and Erika's new home for a house warming party on New Year's Eve. When we left home it was about -20 degrees F. When we arrived at the Flagg home, a little over forty miles away, it was -47 degrees F. North of Cantwell was white-out conditions with blowing snow. Jerome had to come to nearly a complete stop because of the blowing snow. On one part of the highway there are a couple dozen or so snow poles about fourteen feet high on each side of the highway. They have reflectors on them so they are easily seen at night as well as in poor weather. They are a guide for the snow plow to know where the road is as well as a guide for travelers. These are odd looking especially in the summer time. When I first saw them in 1991 I could not imagine what they were for. Since then I have learned how important those poles can be.

Jerome did get the chairs done. He made six, two he gave to Clayton and Erika, the other four are for us. On News Year's Day Gabe and Beth are coming to our place for deep fried turkey and other goodies. We will get to use the new chairs for the first time. I believe there is a coffee table in the makings out in the shop(?).

The events of the new year will have to be saved for my next book. At this time we have had nearly thirteen feet of snow fall since October, 1999, some of it has settled, but a great deal of it remains pilled high, and it is still snowing! Papa Pretty

Bird is waiting to be hand-fed sunflower seeds.

I am truly fortunate to live in Alaska. Many people save for many years to get to visit Alaska, a trip of a lifetime. How many do the same to visit Iowa or North Dakota?

Our home at Colorado Lake, October 18, 1999

Our home at Colorado Lake, December 28, 1999

Jerome at his shop with newly built chairs, December 20, 1999

Jerome shoveling out during snow storm, December 20, 1999

Postscript

January 6, 2000, Jerome and I were in Cantwell, where we counted about forty moose in the river bottoms. This is an unusually high number in an area. Because of the severe winter with large snow-fall, they came from the mountains in search of food. The snow was perhaps at least ten feet deep in the mountains. Moose are a solitary animal, almost always alone except for a cow and calf. Unlike caribou who stay in herds. We saw one moose about 1,500 feet from the highway, it was lying in the deep snow away from trees or brush, as if it had given up. Many of these moose will starve to death, which is sad to see.

By the time this book was ready for printing we had 23 1/2 feet of snowfall!

Jerome by our house, February 3, 2000

Jerome by generator building, February 3, 2000

Author climbing snowbank near her home,
February 7, 2000